HE
HEALED
THEM
ALL

CONTENTS

"... BY HIS WOUNDS YOU HAVE BEEN HEALED."

(1 Peter 2:24 NIV)

Laurie and I encourage you, dear TBN Partner, to get in agreement with God's Word for whatever healing you or a loved one needs. That's why we commissioned the writing of **He Healed Them All: *40 Days of Promise, 40 Days of Miracles***. As you read this devotional, we pray that your faith is strengthened to believe for and receive the salvation and healing that already belong to you in the name of King Jesus. May God bless you!

– Matt and Laurie Crouch

"MIRACLES ARE NOT OPTIONAL."

Jesus ministered from place to place throughout all of the province of Galilee. He taught in the synagogues, preaching the hope of the kingdom realm and healing every kind of sickness and disease among the people. His fame spread everywhere! Many people who were in pain and suffering with every kind of illness were brought to Jesus for their healing—epileptics, paralytics, and those tormented by demonic powers were all set free. Everyone who was brought to Jesus was healed!

This resulted in massive crowds of people following him, including people from Galilee, Jerusalem, the land of Judah, the region of the Ten Cities known as the Decapolis, and beyond the Jordan River. (Matthew 4:23–25)

The New Testament opens with the book of Matthew. In chapter 1, we read the lineage of Jesus, which begins with Abraham, whose wife Sarah's womb was miraculously opened at 90 years of age to give him a son, Isaac. Fascinating, isn't it, that Jesus's lineage is traced back to a healing miracle! The lineage ends with Jesus, *"who is called the 'Anointed One'"* (Matthew 1:16).

Matthew continues by relating the miraculous conception of Jesus, as foretold to Joseph. In chapter 2, after the birth of the Christ child, a group of priests, or *"wise men,"* come to see the newborn King. Jesus and His parents go into hiding while Herod goes on a rampage, killing toddlers in hopes of taking out the promised Messiah.

Fast forward 30 years and we meet John the Baptist, Jesus's cousin, who is preparing the hearts of the people for the coming of the Lord. Enter Jesus, who comes to John to be baptized. *"After his baptism, as Jesus came up out of the water, the heavens were opened and he saw the Spirit of God descending like a dove and settling on him."* (Matthew

3:16). The "Anointed One" had officially been anointed to do what He came to this earth to do. Which was what, exactly?

Pastor Bill Johnson writes in his book, *The Essential Guide to Healing*:

> "For as long as I can remember, the message of the Church has been the salvation of souls. Wonderful evangelistic crusades are organized to bring the multitudes to Jesus. Evangelism is also taken to the streets, as normal people invade our cities and learn to share the good news of God's forgiveness for everyone. Perhaps it is the beauty of that message that has lulled us to sleep concerning the rest of our assignment. It is bigger than that. Jesus clearly taught us that we were to preach the message of the Kingdom to every nation before the end would come (see Matthew 24:14). That message releases the Kingdom through miracles.

> "The message of salvation is contained in the Gospel of the Kingdom. The good news of the Kingdom is the proclamation that God's dominion is in effect now. King-dom. That is, King's domain. The message of the Kingdom is the message of the King's domain that is in effect here and now. And whenever Jesus proclaimed this message, miracles followed. Miracles were the natural result of His dominion being realized. *'Jesus was going through all the cities and villages, teaching in their synagogues and proclaiming the gospel of the kingdom, and healing every kind of disease and every kind of sickness'* (Matthew 9:35 NASB). The right message attracts God's power since He loves to confirm His Word.

> "The message of salvation would not be so incomplete if it were preached as God intended. Today salvation means we can be 'forgiven of sin.' If there were nothing more than this, it would be worth it all. Forgiveness is still the ultimate miracle. But to assert that there is more to the message does not diminish the importance of forgiveness. It is just that God intended more. Jesus said, *'For the Son of Man did not come to destroy men's*

2

lives, but to save them' (Luke 9:56 NASB). The word 'save' in the original Greek language is the word *sozo*. It refers specifically to the forgiveness of sin, the healing of disease and the deliverance from torment. That is salvation. Jesus made the provision needed to save the whole person—spirit (forgiveness), soul (deliverance), and body (healing).

"The Gospel of salvation is meant to touch the whole person." (Johnson, 2011)

After Jesus's baptism in the Holy Spirit, He was empowered in His purpose and immediately set out to share the Gospel message: *"Keep turning away from your sins and come back to God, for heaven's kingdom realm is now accessible"* (Matthew 4:17). And out of that proclamation came healing: *"... He taught in the synagogues, preaching the hope of the kingdom realm and healing every kind of sickness and disease among the people"* (v. 23). Hope, healing, and miracles were always a part of the life and ministry of Jesus.

According to Johnson:

"The Gospel must include miracles to be fully expressed. Miracles are not optional." (Johnson, 2011)

HEALING WALKS IN THE DOOR

Then Jesus went into Peter's home and found Peter's mother-in-law bedridden, severely ill with a fever. The moment Jesus touched her hand she was healed! Immediately she got up and began to make dinner for them.

That evening the people brought to him many who were demonized. And by Jesus only speaking a word of healing over them, they were totally set free from their torment, and everyone who was sick received their healing! In doing this, Jesus fulfilled the prophecy of Isaiah:

> *He put upon himself our weaknesses, and he carried away our diseases and made us well.* (Matthew 8:14–17)

Several methods of healing are seen in these four verses of Matthew 8.

- Jesus heals with **touch**: He laid hands on Peter's mother-in-law and she was healed.

- Jesus heals with **words**: He spoke a word of healing over the demonized and they were set free.

- Jesus heals **instantly**: Scripture says IMMEDIATELY Peter's mother-in-law was able to get up, after being bedridden with a fever.

- Jesus heals **completely**: The demonized weren't just set free—they were TOTALLY set free. Peter's mother-in-law's fever didn't just break, she was able to jump out of bed and get Thanksgiving dinner on the table.

In his personal testimony of healing, Jack Hayford says:

> "Healing does not float down out of the sky or come through the chimney. If it comes to homes, it's more than likely going to walk through the door with you coming to visit someone who's sick. Healing comes because you come with love like Jesus loves. You speak the words of the Lord Jesus. You offer His kindness and faithfulness. There are a lot of different ways the Lord heals. These are four:
>
> 1. When you pray and ask with faith (see John 14:12–13)— The faith is in the Word of God. Jesus says that greater things are going to happen in you than ever happened in His ministry. It's all His power anyway.
>
> 2. When you lay hands on the sick in Jesus' name—"In Jesus' name" is by the authority or privilege we've been given.
>
> 3. When you receive communion and believe—There is healing when we come to the Lord's table.
>
> 4. When you ask elders to anoint with oil (see James 5:14,16)—You need to ask for somebody to come and pray for you. The Bible uses oil as a picture of the Holy Spirit and His being at work with power. We anoint with oil to welcome the power of the Holy Spirit, and the Bible says that the yoke, or what ties people up, shall be broken or destroyed because of the anointing." (Hayford, *www.jackhayford.org/teaching/articles/my-personal-testimony-of-healing/*)

Healing didn't descend like a dove onto Peter's mother-in-law, it walked in the door. When we have the power of the Holy Spirit and the presence of Jesus with us, healing also walks in the door with us when we visit the sick.

Matthew 8:14–17 ends by saying that the prophecy of Isaiah was fulfilled.

Jack Hayford explains:

> "It was foretold that the coming Messiah will heal (Isaiah 53:5): *'But He was wounded for our transgressions, He was bruised for our iniquities; the chastisement for our peace was upon Him, and by His stripes we are healed.'* Chastisement means the beating; He took the beating for us in order that we could be put together. Peace doesn't only mean quietness inside you, but it means completeness or wholeness in all of you. The devil beats on people; circumstances can break them apart. The Bible says that Jesus's suffering was intended to take the place of our suffering. Just as Jesus died for our sins so we could be forgiven, He suffered for our sickness, so we could be healed.

> "Divine healing is not a matter of guesswork. It was prophesied in the Word that God would send a Savior who would not only forgive our sins, but bring healing to the human body. That's the promise God made. The prophecy that was made was fulfilled (see Matthew 8:17). Jesus was not simply healing because He cared about human need, but He was healing because He was keeping a promise that God had made to man centuries earlier. When you ask the Lord to forgive your sins, He does it now because He paid for it a long time ago. When we come to the Lord and ask Him for healing, He is ready to do it now because He provided for it when He suffered for our sicknesses long ago.

> "The apostle Peter, writing to the Church of all history says by His stripes, your healing has already been accomplished (see 1 Peter 2:24). Healing is something that is already paid for. What was foretold was fulfilled, and today, it's for sure: the risen Messiah comes to bring healing to us now." (Hayford, *www.jackhayford.org/ teaching/articles/my-personal-testimony-of-healing/*)

IT'S IN THE BOOK

As Jesus left Capernaum he came upon a tax-collecting station, where a traitorous Jew was busy at his work, collecting taxes for the Romans. His name was Matthew. "Come, follow me," Jesus said to him. Immediately Matthew jumped up and began to follow Jesus.

Later, Jesus went to Matthew's home to share a meal with him. Many other tax collectors and outcasts of society were invited to eat with Jesus and his disciples.

When those known as the Pharisees saw what was happening, they were indignant, and they kept asking Jesus's disciples, "Why would your Master dine with such lowlifes?"

When Jesus overheard this, he spoke up and said, "Healthy people don't need to see a doctor, but the sick will go for treatment." Then he added, "Now you should go and study the meaning of the verse:

I want you to show mercy, not just offer me a sacrifice.

"For I have come to invite the outcasts of society and sinners, not those who think they are already on the right path." (Matthew 9:9–13)

Jesus was clear about the purpose of His ministry: preach the Gospel, heal the sick, raise the dead, cleanse those who have leprosy, and drive out demons. And He was clear that if He was to do all these things, if He was to heal as many as He could and cast out as many demons as He could and preach to as many as who needed to hear the Gospel as He could, then He had to be with the sick, the dead, the leprous, the demon-possessed, and the sinners. Doctors don't focus their energies on healthy people any more than healthy people hang out with doctors. It's the sick that need doctors for healing and doctors need the sick if they are to operate in their calling.

But just as Jesus was criticized for hanging out with sinners, many in the Church today are criticized for their healing ministries. Even though this is the clear calling of the Gospel, many—believers and non-believers alike—have a hard time understanding.

The late John Wimber, pastor of the Vineyard Movement, was well-known for his healing ministries, as well as his unique "calling" into this ministry. He wrote in his book, *The Way In Is the Way On*:

"When I began hearing the Lord regarding praying for the sick, I had no actual proof in my life or ministry that God would back up my actions when I began teaching on the works of the Kingdom. I've often been asked, 'Did you experience a miraculous healing that led you into this ministry?' 'Have you had a visitation from an angel?' 'Did a divine healer lay hands on you and impart his anointing to you?' These kinds of questions presupposed a theology that to participate in Jesus's ministry I needed some kind of spiritual experience to initiate my ministry.

"My response to these kinds of questions was a simple, 'No. It's in the Book, so I do it.' I was obeying Scripture because I believed that if Jesus said it and did it, then I should do it. This is important because it answers a common criticism that some have leveled at others and me.

"Some contend that we start with our experience and then turn to Scripture to support it. The exact opposite was true for me. Instead, I started with the Bible, especially the gospels. I chose to obey the commands of Jesus without knowing whether or not we would see any results. And it was only when I tried to emulate Jesus's words and works in my life that my experience changed.

I did not have a climactic moment of holy electricity that caused me to find texts to support my experience.

"Every week I would teach from Scripture and then I would give an opportunity for people to come forward who needed prayer for healing. At one point, I became completely discouraged. We had been praying for the sick for nine months and had yet to see anyone healed of anything, not even a headache! Some of our friends left the church out of frustration and irritation. I wanted to quit. How could I keep teaching on healing when no results were backing it up?

"It was then I sensed the Lord asking me, 'Do you want to teach my Word or your experience?' I knew the answer. There was no turning back. Whether or not Jesus ever answered our prayers with healing, it was my job to obey His mandate." (Wimber, 2006)

Wimber didn't preach that God wanted to heal people because he'd seen people healed. Wimber didn't preach that God wanted to heal people because he'd been healed himself. Wimber preached that God wanted to heal people because that is what Jesus preached, and that is what Jesus did. Even when Wimber did not see results— some say it was two full years before anyone in his meetings was healed—Wimber continued to preach that Jesus came to forgive our sins and heal our diseases because that's what it says in the Book. Wimber says, "We cannot do or teach less than what is in the Bible."

It isn't our job to heal. It is our job to be obedient. And to trust God no matter what. Wimber goes on to explain:

"When we pray for a person's healing, our goal should be that no matter the outcome—healed or not—that we are to leave him or her feeling more loved by God than before we prayed. One of the ways I express God's love is by showing interest in every aspect of the person's life. Often this means that praying for the sick takes a great deal of time, both in initial and follow-up prayer sessions. However, if it's the person God's interested in,

9

we should then look upon him or her with the love and concern that Jesus has for them." (Wimber, 2006)

Healed or not, a person should feel more loved than before we prayed. Perhaps it is love that heals, more than laying on of hands or anointing with oil. Which explains why Jesus took the time to eat with tax collectors, talk to the woman at the well, see the woman with the issue of blood, and break bread with His disciples. Because love is spelled t-i-m-e.

DAY 4

EXPECT TO BE HEALED

As Jesus left the house, two blind men began following him, shouting out over and over, "Son of David, show us mercy and heal us!" And they followed him right into the house where Jesus was staying. So Jesus asked them, "Do you believe that I have the power to restore sight to your eyes?"

They replied, "Yes Lord, we believe!"

Then Jesus put his hands over their eyes and said, "You will have what your faith expects!" And instantly their eyes opened—they could see! Then Jesus warned them sternly, "Make sure that you tell no one what just happened!" But unable to contain themselves, they went out and spread the news everywhere! (Matthew 9:27–31)

According to a commentary in *The Passion Translation*, these two blind men were the first (besides the wise men at Jesus's birth) to recognize Jesus as King.

"Son of David," they called Him, which was basically the same as saying "Messiah."

"Show us mercy and heal us!" (v. 27) they shouted, because if it was true that He was the King of the Jews, then the prophecy must also be true—that He had come to give sight to the blind.

"Do you believe that I have the power to restore sight to your eyes?" (v. 28) Jesus asked. Do you truly believe? Where is your faith? Is it in me?

"Yes Lord, we believe!" (v. 28). Can't you just feel their excitement? They were hardly able to hold still long enough for Jesus to put His hands over their eyes because they knew—deep in their hearts, they knew—that He had the power to restore their vision.

11

"You will have what your faith expects!" (v. 29) Jesus said.

If there was any doubt that their faith was genuine, it was laid to rest. If they hadn't truly believed, if their faith hadn't fully expected healing, they would not have regained their sight at Jesus's words. But when He declared their faith to be made manifest, *"instantly their eyes opened—they could see!"* (v. 30).

Leon Fontaine taught on his broadcast, *The Spirit Contemporary Life*:

> "Believing is a process that brings us to faith which means we are completely convinced it's mine. Believing is simply taking the Word of God and speaking it, taking the Word of God and seeing your miracle done, finished. What would you act like, what would your life look like when this miracle is done? See it ahead of time. See the prosperity. See the healing. See what it would do to your marriage or home ... whatever it is you have to see the end from the beginning. That is the language of the heart." (Fontaine, "Living A Miraculous Life")

These two blind men were convinced in their hearts that Jesus had the power to give sight to the blind. They envisioned themselves with vision. Long before they ever heard Jesus's voice and followed Him out of Jairus's house (see Matthew 9:18–26, where Jesus raises Jairus's daughter from the dead), they believed that as soon as they could get His attention, they would be healed. Their faith expected a miracle. And with a simple touch and a simple declaration (*"You will have what your faith expects!"*), Jesus gave power to their faith and it was realized.

Fontaine believes, that same faith, that same healing power, is available to us today, by the grace of God:

> "Faith believes that grace—which is His favor—gives it to me—healing, prosperity, blessing, joy, peace—everything you can find a promise for in the Bible, you get it as a favor. Jesus qualifies you for it. He gives you the gift of righteousness so you can receive it." (Fontaine, "Living A Miraculous Life")

These men received healing as a favor from God—*even before Jesus went to the Cross.* How much more should we believe, knowing that Jesus died to give us right standing with God?

What is your faith expecting? As you think about the answer to this question, remember the words of Jesus: *"You will have what your faith expects!"*

DAY 5

JESUS GAVE US AUTHORITY

While they were leaving, some people brought before Jesus a man with a demon spirit who couldn't speak. Jesus cast the demon out of him, and immediately the man began to speak plainly. The crowds marveled in astonishment, saying, "We've never seen miracles like this in Israel!" But the Pharisees kept saying, "The chief of demons is helping him drive out demons." (Matthew 9:32–34)

When Jesus first arrived on the scene, people must have wondered: *Why did He come? What is He doing here?* First John 3:8 says: *"... For this purpose the Son of God was manifested, that He might destroy the works of the devil"* (NKJV). Jesus came to destroy the works of the devil, plain and simple. And when it comes to healing, Pastor Mike Bickle says: "A medical answer will not solve the problem if a demon is causing it." (Bickle, "The Authority of the Believer: Standing in our Healing")

So, what do we know about demonic powers, casting out demons, and taking authority over the devil? Bickle writes:

"Each believer must be taught to receive healing and freedom and then to keep in it by personally standing on the Word. Speaking the Word of God is our weapon and protection against demons. The shield of faith is the consistent confident declaration of the Word against the enemy's attack.

Put on the whole armor of God, that you may be able to stand against the wiles of the devil. We do not wrestle against flesh and blood, but against principalities, against powers ... in the heavenly places. Take up the whole armor of God, that you may be able to withstand in the evil day, and having done all, to stand. Stand ... having girded your

14

waist with truth ... taking the shield of faith with which you will be able to quench all the fiery darts of the wicked one ... Take the sword of the Spirit, which is the word of God ... (Eph. 6:11–17)

"We must **stand** for all the ground we take from the enemy. He will come to take it back by lies. Once a person is delivered, they must learn to **stand** against the devil for themselves. ...

"Principle of the kingdom: The demonstration of the Spirit follows a declaration of a believer. The Spirit moves as the Word is spoken. We resist oppression by rebuking it in Jesus's name.

"The primary way Satan tries to gain access to people is through their mind and body. The degree to which one yields to Satan in these areas determines how much Satan is able to influence him.

"Each person has three parts: We are a spirit, we have a soul and live in a body. Demons can influence or oppress a Christian's body and soul (mind and emotions) without possessing their spirit. There are degrees of oppression. A bad mood or emotional funk can be the direct result of flaming missiles of demonic oppression.

"Our spiritual authority is based on our union with Jesus. The power and benefits that Jesus received as an 'exalted Man' are given us. God gave Jesus to the Church as our Head and who we are as His body or vehicle to express His power to the earth (see Eph. 1:19–23).

"We have been raised to sit with Jesus in heavenly places, thus are given access to God's throne. Our prayers in God's will reach His throne and find approval resulting in the release of power. We must know who we are in Christ and the authority we possess in Jesus. We must take our place of authority in Christ as those seated in heavenly places with Jesus (see Eph. 1:3, 20–22; 2:6).

"At the cross, Jesus as a Man defeated Satan and all demonic principalities and made a public spectacle of them before the audience of heaven, hell, and earth. This victory is finished.

Having disarmed principalities and powers, He made a public spectacle of them, triumphing over them in it [His death and resurrection]. (Col. 2:15)

"Authority is delegated power. An example that is commonly used is that of a police officer who stops a car by the authority of the government, not his own physical power. We use spiritual authority against Satan who seeks to steal, kill, and destroy God's blessing in our life (by fear, addictions, emotional oppression, division, sickness, financial oppression, etc.).

'The thief [Satan] does not come except to steal, and to kill, and to destroy. I have come that they may have life, and that they may have it more abundantly.' (Jn. 10:10)

"We are called to enforce Jesus's authority on earth as His body. Satan's attack against us will continue if we accept it, instead of refusing it or challenging it with our authority in Christ.

Therefore submit to God. Resist the devil and he will flee from you. (Jas 4:7)

"Fear, rejection, and addictive urges are a form of demonic oppression that must be rebuked. If they are allowed to gain dominance in our thinking, they will dominate our life with despair. We must take authority over the spirit of fear. It must not be accepted or allowed to grow.

God has not given us a spirit of fear, but of power and of love and of a sound mind. (2 Tim. 1:7)

"The command of faith doesn't always bring results instantly.

Do not become sluggish, but imitate those who through faith and patience inherit the promises. (Heb. 6:12)

"Our authority is based on what Jesus accomplished, not on our moods, feelings, fervor, or victory.

'Not by [human] might nor by power, but by My Spirit,' Says the LORD of hosts.' (Zech. 4:6)

(Bickle, "The Authority of the Believer: Standing in our Healing")

Jesus cast out demons; and by His authority, believers can continue to cast out demons today. Jesus is the same yesterday, today, and forever. If His purpose 2,000 years ago was to destroy the works of the devil, that will continue to be His purpose until it is complete!

NO LIMIT TO GOD'S POWER

Jesus walked throughout the region with the joyful message of God's kingdom realm. He taught in their meeting houses, and wherever he went he demonstrated God's power by healing every kind of disease and illness.

When he saw the vast crowds of people, Jesus's heart was deeply moved with compassion, because they seemed weary and helpless, like wandering sheep without a shepherd. He turned to his disciples and said, "The harvest is huge and ripe! But there are not enough harvesters to bring it all in. As you go, plead with the Owner of the Harvest to thrust out many more reapers to harvest his grain!" (Matthew 9:35–38)

There is no limit to God's power. He has power to heal *"every kind of disease and illness"* (v. 35). There is nothing outside the realm of His expertise! And He has the power to heal every single person, *"vast crowds of people"* (v. 36). His power doesn't run out! In fact, quite the opposite. Marilyn Hickey writes in her book, *Be Healed*, "When large groups of people come together in agreement to praise and worship the Lord, there is a rich anointing to heal the masses. No situation is too big for the Lord." (Hickey) Scripture says that *"where two or three are gathered together in My name, I am there in the midst of them"* (Matthew 18:20 NKJV). The anointing can actually strengthen and increase with the number of people gathered. Hickey writes:

> "It doesn't matter who you are or where you are, Jesus wants to heal you. It doesn't matter if it's a common cold or a terminal cancer, Jesus wants to heal you. Our Lord is no respecter of persons and He is no respecter of disease. You don't have to be a preacher, a Sunday school teacher, or give half your income to the church to get

ready for healing. You just have to believe that He has enough love, enough compassion, and enough power to do it for you." (Hickey)

Jesus's compassion shines through in Matthew 9. Why did He heal all who came to Him? Because they were like sheep without a shepherd, wandering aimlessly, lost with no direction, helpless. We are God's children, and He is a loving, compassionate Father. Marilyn Hickey gives a great illustration of this in her book:

"If you are a parent, you want your children to be healthy. When they are sick, you never want them to get sicker. You do everything in your power to bring about healing. You take them to the doctor; you give them prescribed medicine; you do whatever is necessary. Parents love their children and want no calamity to overtake them. Loving parents would rather be sick themselves than see their children sick. Most parents would take their child's sickness upon themselves if that were possible. That is exactly what our heavenly Parent did; He took our sickness upon Himself, and then He carried it away." (Hickey)

God is a good, good Father. But God doesn't just heal our physical sicknesses, He heals every area of our lives where there is lack. Marilyn explains:

"There is not one sickness, not one problem, not one impossibility that God cannot turn into a miracle for you. Even if what you need does not exist, your loving heavenly Father is able to bring it into existence, whether it's a new job or a "new" body. Nothing is impossible with our God. Whatever you need, the Lord can supply, even though it may take a miracle. God is able to heal your finances as well as your body. He is able to heal your marriage and change your wayward children. Don't put your confidence in people nor your present circumstances. All that can change in an instant. Put your confidence in God; trust Him. The difference between those who receive their miracle and those who do not is faith. God is not a respecter of persons; He is a respecter of faith." (Hickey)

The people may have been like sheep without a shepherd, but they had enough faith to follow Jesus; and it was that faith that got them healed. Hickey says, "If we are going to be healed, we must first be convinced that it is God's will to heal." She encourages believers, after they are convinced that it is His will to heal, they are to trust Him to work in His way and His timing:

> "Isn't the Lord able to rain gigantic hailstones on His enemies, shake the earth to open prison doors, stop the venom of poisonous snakes, deliver from demons, and rebuke sickness and death? He is not only able, but He has done it before and He can do it again. Don't ever limit the Lord. Believe Him to perform whatever miraculous sign or creative wonder you need. God is unlimited in His authority, unlimited in His power and might, and He is unlimited in His mercy, compassion, and love for you. Always trust Him for the best. When you run out of ideas, He has just begun to think of ways to deliver you!" (Hickey)

Jesus went from place to place, healing every kind of sickness and disease, and every time it looked a little different. His creativity is unlimited in His power to heal!

IN HIM, WE ARE FREE

One Saturday, on the day of rest, Jesus and his disciples were walking through a field of wheat. The disciples were hungry, so they plucked off some heads of grain and rubbed them in their hands to eat. But when some of the Pharisees saw what was happening, they said to him, "Look! Your disciples shouldn't be harvesting grain on the Sabbath!"

Jesus responded, "Haven't you ever read what King David and his men did when they were hungry? They entered the house of God and ate the sacred bread of God's presence, violating the law by eating bread that only the priests were allowed to eat.

"And haven't you read in the Torah that the priests violated the rules of the Sabbath by carrying out their duties in the temple on a Saturday, and yet they are without blame? But I say to you, there is one here who is even greater than the temple. If only you could learn the meaning of the words 'I want compassion more than a sacrifice,' you wouldn't be condemning my innocent disciples. For the Son of Man exercises his lordship over the Sabbath."

Then Jesus left them and went into the synagogue where he encountered a man who had an atrophied, paralyzed hand. The fault-finding Pharisees asked Jesus, "Is it permissible to perform a work of healing on the Sabbath, when no one is supposed to work?" They only asked him this question because they hoped to accuse him of breaking the Jewish laws.

He answered them, "If any of you had a lamb that fell into a ditch on the Sabbath, wouldn't you reach out your hand and lift it out? Isn't a man much more valuable than a lamb? So of course, it's always proper to do miracles, even on the Sabbath."

Then he turned to the man and said, "Hold out your hand!"
And as he stretched it out, it was restored, exactly like the other.

Immediately the Pharisees went out and started to scheme about how they would do away with him. Jesus knew what they were thinking, so he left by another way. Massive crowds followed him from there, and he healed all who were sick. However, he sternly warned them not to tell others or disclose his real identity, in order to fulfill the prophecy of Isaiah:

> *Take a careful look at my servant, my chosen one. I love him dearly and I find all my delight in him. I will breathe my Spirit upon him and he will decree justice to the nations. He will not quarrel or be found yelling in public. He won't brush aside the bruised and broken. He will be gentle with the weak and feeble, until his victory releases justice. And the fame of his name will birth hope among the people.* (Matthew 12:1–21)

When God issued the Ten Commandments, He spent more time talking about the Sabbath than any other commandment:

> *"Remember the Sabbath day by keeping it holy. Six days you shall labor and do all your work, but the seventh day is a sabbath to the LORD your God. On it you shall not do any work, neither you, nor your son or daughter, nor your male or female servant, nor your animals, nor any foreigner residing in your towns. For in six days the LORD made the heavens and the earth, the sea, and all that is in them, but he rested on the seventh day. Therefore the LORD blessed the Sabbath day and made it holy."*
> (Exodus 20:8–11 NIV)

When Moses retold these commandments to the Israelites, he added: *"Remember that you were slaves in Egypt and that the LORD your God brought you out of there with a mighty hand and an outstretched arm. Therefore the LORD your God has commanded you to observe the Sabbath day"* (Deuteronomy 5:15 NIV).

The scribes and Pharisees knew the importance of keeping the Sabbath, and they decided to use this knowledge to test Jesus by pointing to a man with a paralyzed hand and asking Jesus if it was "*lawful*" to heal on the Sabbath.

Joseph Prince taught in one of his sermons at New Creation Church in Singapore: "They were not watching to see if He could heal, but to see if He *would* heal." (Prince J., "Live Healed")

By now, they knew He *could* heal. That wasn't in question. The question was whether He *would* heal, and therefore break the Sabbath law.

Jesus does heal the man's paralyzed hand, but not before He tells the Pharisees that they missed the lesson on love and compassion in Sunday School, and therefore were missing out on the freedom that God intended through establishing the Sabbath. Jesus never says He disagrees with the law, in fact, quite the opposite:

> "*If you think I've come to set aside the law of Moses or the writings of the prophets, you're mistaken. I have come to fulfill and bring to perfection all that has been written. Indeed, I assure you, as long as heaven and earth endure, not even the smallest detail of the Law will be done away with until its purpose is complete. So whoever violates even the least important of the commandments, and teaches others to do so, will be the least esteemed in the realm of heaven's kingdom. But whoever obeys them and teaches their truths to others will be greatly esteemed in the realm of heaven's kingdom. For I tell you, unless your lives are more pure and full of integrity than the religious scholars and the Pharisees you will never experience the realm of heaven's kingdom.*" (Matthew 5:17–20)

It is for freedom that Christ set us free, "*not partially, but completely and wonderfully free!*" (Galatians 5:1).

IN HIM, WE HAVE VICTORY OVER THE ENEMY

Then a man was brought before Jesus who had a demon spirit that made him both blind and unable to speak. Jesus healed him instantly, and he could see and talk again! The crowds went wild with amazement as they witnessed this miracle. And they kept saying to one another, "Could this man be the Messiah?"

But when the Pharisees overheard what the people were saying about the miracle, they said, "He casts out demons by the power of Satan, the prince of demons!"

Now, Jesus supernaturally perceived their thoughts and motives, so he confronted them by telling them this parable:

"Any kingdom that fights against itself will end up in ruins. And any family or community splintered by strife will fall apart. So if Satan casts out Satan, he is making war on himself. How then could his kingdom survive? So if Satan empowers me to cast out demons, who empowers your exorcists to cast them out? Go ask them, for what they do proves you're wrong in your accusations. On the other hand, if I drive out demons by the power of the Spirit of God, then the end of Satan's kingdom has come! Who would dare enter the house of a mighty man and steal his property? First he must be overpowered and tied up by one who is stronger than he. Then his entire house can be plundered and every possession stolen.

"So join with me, for if you're not on my side you are against me. And if you refuse to help me gather the spoils, you are making things worse. This is why I warn you, for God will

*forgive people for every sin and blasphemy they have com-
mitted except one. There is no forgiveness for the sin of
blasphemy against the Holy Spirit. If anyone speaks evil of
me, the Son of Man, he can be forgiven; but if anyone con-
temptuously speaks against the Holy Spirit, it will never be
forgiven, now or ever!"* (Matthew 12:22–32)

The themes of the "Kingdom of God" and "Satan's kingdom" are
prevalent in this passage, and in any discussion of healing. Pastor
John Wimber expounds on these themes:

> "In the Old Testament, the Kingdom of God was related
> to Jewish messianic expectation. It was connected with
> Jewish eschatology, their hope for the future. In his-
> toric Judaism, the Kingdom of God was understood in a
> nationalistic sense. The people carried a military hope—
> geographic, and political—that a nationalistic kingdom
> might once again be established. It would be a future
> empire just like the rule of King David. The first cen-
> tury Jews were looking for another king like King David,
> an anointed Messiah to lead them to political power
> through military might.

> "When Jesus spoke of the Kingdom of God, most people
> thought of a literal kingdom led by the Jewish people.
> John 6:15 clearly supports this: *'Jesus, knowing that they
> intended to come and make Him king by force, withdrew
> again to a mountain by Himself.'* This was also the longing
> of the disciples, even after being with Jesus for years. Acts
> 1:6 says, *'So when they met together, they asked Him, 'Lord,
> are you at this time going to restore the kingdom to Israel?'*

> "Jesus was not talking about a temporal, nationalistic
> kingdom, nor was He speaking solely of a futuristic, pie-
> in-the-sky heavenly kingdom, as the term 'Kingdom
> of God' came to mean among scholars in the intertes-
> tamental period. He was announcing the fact that He
> was establishing His rule on this earth. No longer would
> Satan have complete dominion over the earth and its
> inhabitants—Jesus had come with one main purpose in

mind: to destroy the activity of Satan in the world. Two of the ways Jesus did this was to heal the sick and cast out demons. The battle was fought over the ownership of human beings. We find instances of conflict between Jesus and Satan concerning hunger (see John 6); natural catastrophes (see Mark 4:35); sickness (see Luke 7:21); and death (see Luke 7:11).

"In all these battles, Jesus was, and continues to be the victor. In Matthew 12:22–31, Jesus makes it clear that the struggle in which He is engaged is not a civil war within a kingdom. It is rather a battle between the Kingdom of God and the kingdom of the devil.

"Perhaps nothing is more prevalent in the Gospels than the concept of the Kingdom of God. For example, in the beginning of the Gospel of Mark we read, after John was put in prison, Jesus went into Galilee, proclaiming the good news of God. *"The time has come,"* He said. *"The Kingdom of God is near. Repent and believe the good news!"* (Mark 1:14–15). In Matthew 4:23, prior to the beginning of a long teaching session, Matthew summarized Jesus's ministry in Galilee as involving three things: *'teaching in their synagogues, preaching the good news of the kingdom, and healing every disease and sickness among the people.'*

"In Matthew 10:7, after Jesus gave the disciples authority to cast out demons and to *heal the sick,* he instructs them to preach *'the Kingdom of heaven is near,'* then *'heal the sick, raise the dead, cleanse those who have leprosy, and drive out demons'* (v.8). The term 'Kingdom' was always on Jesus's tongue.

"And Jesus makes it clear that the battle is between the Kingdom of God and the kingdom of darkness. It is quite obvious that cosmic war has been declared. Jesus has come to invade Satan's kingdom and defeat it. Jesus also gave this mission of bringing in the reign of God to the disciples. *'When you enter a town and are welcomed, eat what is set before you. Heal the sick who are there and tell them 'the kingdom of God is near you''* (Luke 10:8–9).

"When Jesus left the earth, He told the disciples that they would be empowered to carry on the mission that He had begun. This included, healing the sick (spiritually, physically, and emotionally), and expelling demons. All this takes power, and that's what He promised in Acts 1:8, *'But you will receive power when the Holy Spirit comes upon you, and you will be my witnesses in Jerusalem, and in all Judea and Samaria, and to the ends of the earth.'*

"What exactly is 'kingdom ministry'? Luke gives a glimpse into Jesus's own self-perception. At Jesus's coronation address He announced His kingly agenda:

'The Spirit of the Lord is on me, because He has anointed me to preach good news to the poor. He has sent me to proclaim freedom for the prisoners and recovery of sight for the blind, to release the oppressed, to proclaim the year of the Lord's favor.' (Luke 4:18–19 NIV)

"In the gospels we find Jesus's action plan for Spirit-empowered ministry: Jesus proclaimed the release of the poor and poor in spirit, declared freedom to prisoners both literal and those bound in sin and darkness; He cast out demons, healed the sick, and mentored disciples to do the same.

"Jesus proclaimed and demonstrated God's right to rule creation as He destroyed the works of Satan (see 1 John 3:8). He equipped followers and promised that they too would do what he did because *'everyone who is fully trained will be like his teacher'* (see Luke 6:40; Matthew 28:16–20; John 14:12–14). I view this process of kingdom ministry as a continuum." (Wimber, 2006)

How powerful it is that every time a person is healed, every time evil is cast out, there is a victory over Satan's kingdom and a win for the Kingdom of God!

MOVED WITH COMPASSION

On hearing this [that John the Baptist had been beheaded], *Jesus slipped away privately by boat to be alone. But when the crowds discovered he had sailed away, they emerged from all the nearby towns and followed him on foot. So when Jesus landed he had a huge crowd waiting for him. Seeing so many people, his heart was deeply moved with compassion toward them, so he healed all the sick who were in the crowd.* (Matthew 14:13–14)

Jesus's heart was tender. He had just learned of His cousin's death. John, who had baptized Him, who had prepared the way for Him, and whose birth had been an example of God's extravagant power to heal, had just been beheaded. John's birth, like the child Isaac way back in the family tree, was the result of God healing the womb of Elizabeth. John had been given to Elizabeth and Zechariah late in life, just as Isaac had been birthed by Abraham and Sarah in their old age.

Jesus needed time alone, time to pray, time to be with His Father. He didn't have long, but it seemed to have been long enough. When He reached land again, Jesus's tender heart was *"deeply moved with compassion"* toward the people, and He *"healed all the sick who were in the crowd."* Every last one of them.

Marilyn Hickey writes in her book, *Be Healed*:

"Many times in the New Testament we read that Jesus looked upon the people with compassion before He healed them. Compassion mixed with faith is a powerful combination. What moved Jesus to heal? Over and over the Word says compassion moved Him to heal the sick and deliver those who were demonized. The Greek meaning for *compassion* is 'to be deeply stirred or moved from within.' Quite literally Jesus was moved with compassion. When Jesus healed the leper who fell at His feet begging to be healed, the plight of the man caused Jesus to be moved with compassion; and He expressed His will by healing the man. (See Mark 1:40–42.) I must add that the man had faith to be healed. If God's compassion were the only requirement for healing, every person alive would be well and healthy. Yet if we have the faith, God always has the compassion.

"It isn't difficult for people to have compassion on those who are sick; but when individuals demonstrate demonic activity, people are more often moved with fear or disgust rather than compassion. However, this was never Jesus's response to the demonized; He always responded with compassion. After delivering the man of Gadara who had a legion of demons, Jesus told the man to go home to his friends and tell them of the great thing the Lord had done for him because He had compassion on him. (See Mark 5:19.)

"Jesus was moved with compassion when He saw the weary multitudes who were scattered as sheep without a shepherd (see Matthew 9:36). Jesus's compassion moved Him to heal the sick among those multitudes of people, and compassion moved Jesus to feed a hungry crowd more than once. The compassion of our Lord caused Him to give sight to two blind men from Jericho, and compassion for a widow woman who had lost her son caused Jesus to stop a funeral procession and raise the young man from the dead (see Luke 7:13).

"Many, many times the writers of the gospels recorded the compassion of Jesus which moved Him to continually minister deliverance to those oppressed by sickness and demons. Jesus Himself, in telling the story of the prodigal son, emphasized the compassion of this young man's father in welcoming him back home and reinstating him to the position of son and heir; which the prodigal had forfeited (see Luke 15:20). Do you realize that Jesus is illustrating the love of our heavenly Father for His way-

29

ward children? Without the anointing of the Holy Spirit, Jesus could have healed no one; so, obviously, the Holy Spirit is just as compassionate as both the Father and the Son. I believe compassion is the 'emotion' of love which activates God's love.

"Does God wants His compassion to flow through you just as it flowed through Jesus? Absolutely. If you do not have compassion for people, then you are not going to be effective in ministering to others. Jesus spoke to every believer when He said:

'Verily, verily, I say unto you, He that believeth on me, the works that I do shall he do also; and greater works than these shall he do; because I go unto my Father.' (John 14:12 KJV)

"Look at this! The same Holy Spirit Who empowered Jesus has come to reside in you, and He is able to perform even greater works through the members of Christ's body— when we are moved with His compassion:

For ye had compassion of me in my bonds, and took joy-fully the spoiling of your goods, knowing in yourselves that ye have in heaven a better and an enduring substance. (Hebrews 10:34 KJV)

Finally, be ye all of one mind, having compassion one of another, love as brethren, be pitiful, be courteous. (1 Peter 3:8 KJV)" (Hickey)

Jesus's "compassions never fail. They are new every morning; great is your [His] faithfulness" (Lamentations 3:22–23 NIV). And every-thing that the Son has, we have as heirs to the promise. Faith and compassion put together result in mighty works! Great is His faith-fulness to us.

YOU DON'T HAVE TO BEG

As soon as the people were fed, Jesus told his disciples to get into their boat and to go to the other side of the lake while he stayed behind to dismiss the people. After the crowds dispersed, Jesus went up into the hills to pray. And as night fell he was there praying alone with God.

But the disciples, who were now in the middle of the lake, ran into trouble, for their boat was tossed about by the high winds and heavy seas.

At about four o'clock in the morning, Jesus came to them, walking on the waves! When the disciples saw him walking on top of the water, they were terrified and screamed, "A ghost!"

Then Jesus said, "Be brave and don't be afraid. I am here!"

Peter shouted out, "Lord, if it's really you, then have me join you on the water!"

"Come and join me," Jesus replied.

So Peter stepped out onto the water and began to walk toward Jesus. But when he realized how high the waves were, he became frightened and started to sink. "Save me, Lord!" he cried out.

Jesus immediately stretched out his hand and lifted him up and said, "What little faith you have! Why would you let doubt win?"

And the very moment they both stepped into the boat, the raging wind ceased. Then all the disciples crouched down before him and worshiped Jesus. They said in adoration, "You are truly the Son of God!"

After they crossed over and landed at Gennesaret, the people living there quickly recognized who he was. They were quick to spread the news throughout the surrounding region that Jesus had come to them. So they brought him all their sick, begging him to let them touch the fringe of his robe. And everyone who touched it was instantly healed! (Matthew 14:22–36)

More than once in Scripture we see the disciples lose their peace in the midst of a storm. In the passage above, Jesus is on land when the storm hits. He has compassion on His disciples, being tossed by the waves, so He walks out to them on the water. If they were afraid before, they are doubly afraid now. They think He is a ghost and start screaming in fear. Jesus issues His most common command: *"Do not be afraid"* (v. 27). Peter is momentarily empowered with confidence. He bravely tells Jesus what to do: *"Lord, if it's really you, then have me join you on the water!"* (v. 28). Jesus replies, *"Come"* (v. 29). Peter steps out in faith, but then takes His eyes off Jesus—his peace—and instead focuses on his fears. It was Jesus's touch, how He *"immediately stretched out his hand and lifted him up"* (v. 31), that saved Peter from drowning and caused the winds to cease. *"What little faith you have!"* Jesus chided (v.31).

Immediately following this encounter, we see countless others healed simply by touching *"the fringe of his robe. And everyone who touched it was instantly healed!"* (v. 36). In that same verse, but before they were healed, Matthew says that they were "begging" Jesus to let them touch Him. Peter begged Jesus to save him. Then the people begged Jesus to heal their friends and family.

Randy Clark writes in his book, *The Essential Guide to Healing*: "To beg God to heal is to assume you have more mercy than He does." (Johnson, 2011)

Ouch!

Yet the Gospels are full of begging. In Luke 4, the disciples begged Jesus to heal Simon Peter's mother-in-law. In Luke 5, a leper fell at

Jesus's feet and begged to be made clean. In Luke 8, Jairus begged Jesus to heal his daughter. In Luke 9, a father begs the disciples and then Jesus to cast a demon out of his son.

Begging wasn't just a New Testament phenomenon. Regularly in the book of Psalms we see David begging:

Every day I beg for your help. Can't you see my tears? My eyes are swollen with weeping. My arms are wide, longing for mercy, but you're nowhere to be found. (Psalm 88:9)

God, I'm crying out to you! I lift up my voice boldly to beg for your mercy. (Psalm 142:1)

David's pleas show us how desperate we appear and how desperate we are when we beg. We've come to the end of ourselves and said, "There's nothing left to do but pray." We've tried everything else and none of it has worked. And precisely because we've relegated prayer to our last line of defense, we feel desperate. But we don't have to beg, and we won't get in this desperate place if we go to God in His mercy first!

When you get a revelation of Who God is and an understanding that it is always God's will to heal, you will no longer resort to begging. You won't have to beg for mercy. You won't have to list all the wonderful qualities about the person who is sick, as if being a good person "qualifies" one for healing. Because you will know that it is God's will to heal. Always.

God wants to heal everyone. He wants to heal the "Peters" of the world who feel like they are drowning. He heals the ones with faith that can move mountains and the ones who need help in their unbelief. No matter the method or circumstances, those who come to Him on the water and those who touch the hem of His robe, He wants to heal. Healing is part of who He is. With a simple touch, He heals everyone who comes to Him.

No one has more mercy than God. No one wants to see your loved ones healed more than Him. You don't have to beg for what is already yours through the finished work of Jesus: *by His wounds, you ARE healed* (see Isaiah 53:5).

BE PERSISTENT IN ASKING

Then Jesus left and went north into the non-Jewish region of Lebanon. He encountered there a Canaanite woman who screamed out to him, "Lord, Son of David, show mercy to me! My daughter is horribly afflicted by a demon that torments her." But Jesus never answered her. So his disciples said to him, "Why do you ignore this woman who is crying out to us?"

Jesus said, "I've only been sent to the lost sheep of Israel." But she came and bowed down before him and said, "Lord, help me!"

Jesus responded, "It's not right for a man to take bread from his children and throw it out to the dogs."

"You're right, Lord," she replied. "But even puppies get to eat the crumbs that fall from the prince's table."

Then Jesus answered her, "Dear woman, your faith is strong! What you desire will be done for you." And at that very moment, her daughter was instantly set free from demonic torment. (Matthew 15:21–28)

When reading the story of the Syro-Phoenician woman, it almost appears that we will have our first example of Jesus NOT healing someone who asks for it. But Pastor Mike Bickle says, "Jesus knows He is going to answer her, but He is drawing her faith out so He can use her as an example." (Bickle, "Defining True Discipleship")

As Jesus and His disciples were walking by the Syro-Phoenician woman—a Gentile—she *"screamed out to him"* (v. 22). She screams! *"But Jesus never answered her"* (v. 23). Jesus ignored her. IGNORED HER! It's incredulous.

Even the disciples were shocked. *"Why do you ignore this woman who is crying out to us?"* (v. 23) they asked.

Jesus had been seen talking to a Samaritan woman at the well. He touched lepers. He healed on the Sabbath. He ate with tax collectors. He raised people from the dead. Why would He ignore this woman's cry for help? This doesn't sound right coming from the man who told the parable of the Good Samaritan. Wasn't this Gentile woman His neighbor too?

"I've only been sent to the lost sheep of Israel," Jesus finally says (v. 24). So He goes from ignoring her to straight up refusing her.

She stops screaming, but now she is at His feet, begging for Him to intervene for her daughter. She refuses to be denied. She won't let go. She will beg and beg until her daughter is healed!

"It's not right for a man to take bread from his children and throw it out to the dogs," Jesus says (v.26). First He ignores her, then He refuses her, and now He insults her.

In Jesus's day, Gentiles were known as "dogs," and Jews as the children of Israel. These are the *"children"* Jesus speaks of, and the *"bread"* is the power to heal. Pastor Mike Bickle explains:

> "Jesus taught us to pray, '*Give us this day, our daily bread*' (Mt. 6:11). Part of our daily bread, the Father's bread for His children, according to Jesus, is healing. He gives us daily bread; He provides for our needs physically with actual food and money. He gives us daily bread in terms of direction. He gives us daily bread through inspiring our hearts in grace to walk in holiness and intimacy and revelation.

> "He directs us; He corrects us. There are many dimensions of bread God promises as a Father to give His children on a daily basis.

> "Jesus tells us a child cannot produce bread; nor does a child try to produce bread under the care of the Father.

A child comes innocently and full of confidence: 'Father, I'm hungry, I need lunch.' It never crosses their minds that the Father won't feed them in that day if the relationship is healthy.

"Jesus puts the healing into that context, into the normal, open-handed provision of God the Father.

"The little four-or-five-year old child doesn't have a second thought about whether it was in the heart of the Father to give them bread that day or not. Most 4-year olds aren't going to go up and say, 'Dad, what do you think? Is lunch on the menu today? I mean, is that on the agenda? Are you going to feed us today?' Four-year olds don't do that! It's, 'Hey, I'm hungry, give me a hamburger.' They're going full-steam ahead.

"Jesus is putting healing into the category of what a child would expect their Father to minister on a routine, daily basis. Jesus says, '*It is not good*'—this is powerful, it's negative. This is a negative thing. He's saying, 'It is not good to give the healing ministry, that daily flow of healing, to the dogs—to throw it down to the dogs.'" (Bickle, "Defining True Discipleship")

In other words, Jesus is telling the woman that because she isn't a Jew, she hasn't inherited the right to healing.

"*You're right, Lord,*" she replied (v. 27). Notice that she doesn't respond to Him as "*Lord, Son of David,*" like she did in verse 22. "Lord, Son of David" is a distinctly Jewish term, identifying Jesus as the Messiah. That title was insider language. By leaving out that title, she was accepting that she was not among the children of Israel, yet she also wasn't willing to give up on her own child.

"*But even puppies get to eat the crumbs that fall from the prince's table*" (v. 27). I want the crumbs, she said. And Jesus replied: "*Dear woman, your faith is strong! What you desire will be done for you*" (v. 28).

Jesus had seemingly ignored, rejected, and insulted the woman, but not in His heart. He knew all along He was going to heal her daughter, but first He wanted her faith to shine for all to see. Bickle says:

> "There are times in our relationship with the Lord that we are seemingly ignored, seemingly refused, even insulted—but the Lord keeps pointing to the Syro-Phoenician woman and saying, *'Be like her. I want you to be fully accepting and fully expecting. Accepting of everyone who comes to my table and expecting miracles.'"* (Bickle, "Defining True Discipleship")

Paul writes, in Romans 1:16 (NIV): *"For I am not ashamed of the gospel, because it is the power of God that brings salvation to everyone who believes: first to the Jew, then to the Gentile."* Salvation belongs to EVERYONE who believes. When the Syro-Phoenician woman refused to give up, *"her daughter was instantly set free"* (v. 28).

IMITATE JESUS

After leaving Lebanon, Jesus went to Lake Galilee and climbed a hill nearby and sat down. Then huge crowds of people streamed up the hill, bringing with them the lame, blind, deformed, mute, and many others in need of healing. They laid them at Jesus's feet and he healed them all.

And the crowds marveled with rapture and amazement, astounded over the things they were witnessing with their own eyes! The lame were walking, the mute were speaking, the crippled were made well, and the blind could see. For three days everyone celebrated the miracles as they exalted and praised the God of Israel! (Matthew 15:29–31)

Randy Clark writes in the book that he co-authored with Bill Johnson, *The Essential Guide to Healing*:

"The clearest revelation of God is His Son, Jesus. Paul said in Colossians 2:9, 'For in Christ all the *fullness of the Deity lives in bodily form.*' The writer of Hebrews said, *'The Son is the radiance of God's glory and the exact representation of his being'* (Hebrews 1:3). Since the Son is the exact representation of God and the fullness of deity lived in Him, it seems proper to me to believe that what we saw Jesus do is the will of God. He revealed God's heart, manifested God's power, and demonstrated God's love, especially through His ministry of healing and deliverance. And not just the apostles, but 'we' are called to be God's co-workers, co-laboring with God." (Johnson, 2011)

Clark goes on to write, "it seems proper to me to believe that what we saw Jesus do is the will of God." Scripture confirms this:

So Jesus said, "I speak to you timeless truth. The Son is not able to do anything from himself or through my own initiative. I only do the works that I see the Father doing, for the Son does the same works as his Father.

"Because the Father loves his Son so much, he always reveals to me everything that he is about to do. And you will all be amazed when he shows me even greater works than what you've seen so far! For just like the Father has power to raise the dead, the Son will raise the dead and give life to whomever he wants." (John 5:19–21)

Jesus says that everything He did was in imitation of God, the Father. Just as we learn by watching our parents, Jesus learned by watching His Holy Parent. Then, based on the parts of Jesus's life recorded in Scripture, we know that God's work is to heal— *"the lame were walking, the mute were speaking, the crippled were made well, and the blind could see"* (Matthew 15:31)—and to resurrect— *"For just like the Father has power to raise the dead, the Son will raise the dead and give life to whomever he wants"* (John 5:21).

As heirs to the Kingdom and co-laborers with God (see 1 Corinthians 3:9), we are called to carry out His will here on earth: *"For whoever does the will of God is my brother, my sister, and my mother!"* (Mark 3:35).

If we know that we are to carry out God's will here on earth, and we know that God's will is to heal because we saw it demonstrated in the life and ministry of Jesus, why are there so many unbelieving believers?

Randy Clark has several theories. One theory cites the writings of Augustine (354-430 AD), one of the strongest leaders of the western Church. Clark says:

"Augustine's writings eventually moved the Church to a blueprint worldview—an understanding that everything in life happens due to the predetermined will of God. This caused a shift in the thinking of the Church regarding healing. Now, instead of believing that sickness was brought on by the devil (who ought to be resisted), people believed that God brought on sickness for a person's spiritual sanctification. Therefore, to pray against an illness could be viewed as resisting God. Instead of praying for healing, believers began to pray for discernment about why God might have brought sickness or disease into someone's life." (Johnson, 2011)

Clark is adamant that this understanding of sickness and disease is not biblical. Jesus said: "*A thief has only one thing in mind—he wants to steal, slaughter, and destroy. But I have come to give you everything in abundance, more than you expect—life in its fullness until you overflow!*" (Jn. 10:10). It is the devil who steals your health in an attempt to destroy your life, not God teaching you a lesson. God is the giver of "*life in its fullness.*" Too many believers have missed out on their healing by believing false doctrine.

Another reason that Clark believes Christians question whether healing is for today is that:

"... healings, miracles, and the dead being raised came to be used as evidence of true doctrine or the deity of Christ. This evidential function should be seen as a secondary purpose of the gifts, not their primary purpose. The primary purpose of healings and miracles is the demonstration of the Gospel and the goodness of God." (Johnson, 2011)

If the primary purpose of healing was to prove that Jesus was who He said He was, then we as His followers would not be expected to live out this same calling. However, healing miracles are not primarily a proof-text for Jesus's divinity. Jesus performed miracles of healing first and foremost because God promised health and wholeness to His children, and God is a keeper of His promises. As co-workers with God, we are expected to do His will by doing what Jesus did: "*these miracle signs will accompany those who believe: ... they will lay hands on the sick and heal them*" (Mark 16:17–18).

THE POWER OF HIS ANOINTING

One day, Jesus came from the Galilean village of Nazareth and had John immerse him in the Jordan River. The moment Jesus rose up out of the water, John saw the heavenly realm split open, and the Holy Spirit descended like a dove and rested upon him. At the same time, a voice spoke from heaven, saying:

> *"You are my Son, my cherished one, and my greatest delight is in you!"*

Immediately after this he was compelled by the Holy Spirit to go into an uninhabited desert region. He remained there in the wilderness for forty days, enduring the ordeals of Satan's tests. He encountered wild animals, but also angels who appeared and ministered to his needs.

Later on, after John the Baptizer was arrested, Jesus went back into the region of Galilee and preached the wonderful gospel of God's kingdom realm. His message was this: "At last the fulfillment of the age has come! It is time for the realm of God's kingdom to be experienced in its fullness! Turn your lives back to God and put your trust in the hope-filled gospel!"

As Jesus was walking along the shore of Lake Galilee, he noticed two brothers fishing: Simon and Andrew. He watched them as they were casting their nets into the sea and said to them, "Come follow me and I will transform you into men who catch people instead of fish!"

Immediately they dropped their nets and left everything behind to follow Jesus. Walking a little farther, Jesus found two other brothers sitting in a boat, along with their father,

41

mending their nets. Their names were Jacob and John, and their father Zebedee. Jesus immediately walked up to them and invited the two brothers to become his followers. At once, Jacob and John dropped their nets, stood up, left their father in the boat with the hired men, and followed Jesus.

Then Jesus and his disciples went to Capernaum, and he immediately started teaching on the Sabbath day in the synagogue. The people were awestruck and overwhelmed by his teaching, because he taught in a way that demonstrated God's authority, which was quite unlike the religious scholars.

Suddenly, during the meeting, a demon-possessed man screamed out, "Hey! Leave us alone! Jesus the victorious, I know who you are. You're God's Holy One and you have come to destroy us!"

Jesus rebuked him, saying, "Silence! You are bound! Come out of him!"

The man's body shook violently in spasms, and the demon hurled him to the floor until it finally came out of him with a deafening shriek! The crowd was awestruck and unable to stop saying among themselves, "What is this new teaching that comes with such authority? With merely a word he commands demons to come out and they obey him!"

So the reports about Jesus spread like wildfire throughout every community in the region of Galilee. (Mark 1:9–28)

Jesus is merciful. Jesus is loving. Jesus has compassion. But Jesus is not soft. Jesus taught with authority. He had command over demons. People were astonished. And according to Marilyn Hickey, it's all because of the anointing:

> "The Father heals because He is merciful and compassionate, and the Son heals because He does what the Father does. However, Jesus doesn't heal just by the Father's love and compassion; He heals by the anointing.

"The Word says Jesus didn't heal the sick until after He was anointed with the Holy Spirit. (See Mark 1:10–11.)

"Jesus was endued with power from the Spirit of God; that power or anointing was what healed and delivered. Did you know the Father promised the same anointing for those who are born again? Jesus, referring to this anointing as the baptism with the Holy Ghost, commanded that every believer receive it. That anointing came for the first time on the day of Pentecost; and Peter afterward declared the same experience is for us, our children, and to all that are afar off, even as many as the Lord our God shall call. (See Acts 1:4–5, 8; 2:1–4, 38–39.)

"The anointing brings healing because the anointing breaks the yoke of Satan's bondage:

And it shall come to pass in that day, that his burden shall be taken away from off thy shoulder, and his yoke from off thy neck, and the yoke shall be destroyed because of the anointing. (Isaiah 10:27 KJV)

"The apostle Paul was very much aware that it was the anointing that gave him the power to accomplish anything for God. In Romans 15:17–19 Paul carefully gave the Spirit of God credit for any and all of the mighty signs and wonders that were manifested through him as he preached the gospel.

"God always wants to confirm His Word with healing and deliverance, evident products of the power and anointing of the Holy Spirit. The Lord yearns for you to receive His anointing and to work miracles through your hands. He has promised believers that they shall lay hands on the sick and they (the sick) shall recover. Quoting Jesus, Mark wrote:

And these signs shall follow them that believe; in my name shall they cast out devils; they shall speak with new tongues; they shall take up serpents; and if they drink any deadly thing, it shall not hurt them; they shall lay hands on the sick, and they shall recover. (Mark 16:17–18 KJV)

"The anointing of the Holy Spirit does much more than heal bodies as the above scripture attests. It breaks every yoke and enables us to walk, not only in health, but in full vigor." (Hickey)

The Holy Spirit descended like a dove (see Mark 1:10), but not to give Jesus soft hands. The Holy Spirit anointed Jesus with power, authority, and a charge to break yokes, cast out demons, and restore humanity to its proper order. There is power in the anointing!

LISTEN TO THE HOLY SPIRIT

They arrived at the other side of the lake, at the region of the Gerasenes. As Jesus stepped ashore, a demon-possessed madman came out of the graveyard and confronted him. The man had been living there among the tombs of the dead, and no one was able to restrain him, not even with chains. For every time they attempted to chain his hands and feet with shackles, he would snap the chains and break the shackles in pieces. He was so strong that no one had the power to subdue him. Day and night he could be found lurking in the cemetery or in the vicinity, shrieking and mangling himself with stones!

When he saw Jesus from a distance, he ran to him and threw himself down before him, screaming out at the top of his lungs, "Leave me alone, Jesus, Son of the Most High God! Swear in God's name that you won't torture me!" (For Jesus had already said to him, "Come out of that man, you demon spirit!")

Jesus said to him, "What is your name?"

"Mob," he answered. "They call me Mob because there are thousands of us in his body!" He begged Jesus repeatedly not to expel them out of the region.

Nearby there was a large herd of pigs feeding on the hillside. The demons begged him, "Send us into the pigs. Let us enter them!"

So Jesus gave them permission, and the demon horde immediately came out of the man and went into the pigs! This caused the herd to rush madly down the steep slope and fall into the lake, drowning about two thousand pigs! Depending *on weight, the cost of two thousand live pigs today could be as much as $250,000. The economic cost to the community over the loss of this herd was significant.*

Now, the herdsmen fled to the nearby villages, telling everyone what they saw as they ran through the countryside, and everyone came out to see what had happened. When they found Jesus, they saw the demonized man sitting there, properly clothed and in his right mind. Seeing what had happened to the man who had thousands of demons, the people were terrified. Those who had witnessed this miracle reported the news to the people and included what had happened to the pigs. Then they asked Jesus to leave their region.

And as Jesus began to get into the boat to depart, the man who had been set free from demons asked him, "Could I go with you?" Jesus answered, "No," but said to him, "Go back to your home and to your family and tell them what the Lord has done for you. Tell them how he had mercy on you."

So the man left and went into the region of Jordan and parts of Syria to tell everyone he met about what Jesus had done for him, and all the people marveled! (Mark 5:1–20)

Jesus's ministry was not only to heal the sick, but also to cast out demons. There are several scriptures that cite specific examples of Jesus casting out demons, but this one always stands out. For one, the possessed man is seen running about naked (see Luke 8:27); and also because of the name of the demon: *"Legion ... for we are many"* (v.9 NIV); thirdly, because Jesus takes out these demons by sending them into pigs that then drown themselves.

Peter Lawrence writes in his book, *The Spirit Who Speaks:*

"Jesus appears to have known the identity of most of His spiritual enemies. In the wilderness He commanded Satan to go by name, and he left (Matt. 4:10–11); He asked Legion his name (Mark 5:9; Luke 8:30); He cast out a 'deaf and mute spirit' (Mark 9:25); and a demon that was mute (Luke 11:14); He dealt with a demon that caused a man to

46

be blind and dumb (Matt. 12:22); and He recognized that *'a daughter of Abraham'* whom He healed had been crippled by a spirit for eighteen years (Luke 13:11,16).

"Although Jesus was in His very nature fully God and fully man, the Gospels present Him as a man filled with the Spirit, anointed for ministry, meaning we can do even *'greater things'* (John 14:12) as we continue that ministry. It may have been a gift of discernment that enabled Jesus to recognize a demon or its manifestations in the person, or it may have been a direct word from God in His spirit, but Jesus did seem to know the identity of demons on a number of occasions, and not all were immediately obvious. He certainly knew what they did and how to get rid of them." (Lawrence, 2011)

Jesus knew what this *"legion"* of demons was doing to the man, and He knew how to cast them out. Interestingly, Jesus listens to the demons when they ask Him not to send them directly to hell (see Luke 8:31), but demons are from Satan so Jesus never intended on allowing them to remain on Earth. He sent them into the pigs, and then the evil-possessed pigs drowned.

According to Lawrence, when it comes to casting out demons, there is no one-size-fits-all remedy.

"When Saul had an evil spirit, David ministered to him with music (1 Sam. 16:23); God used Peter's shadow (Acts 5:15) and Paul's handkerchiefs (Acts 19:12); Jesus initially resisted the approach of a Syro-Phoenician woman (Mark 7:24–30), took time questioning a boy's father (Mark 9:14–29), asked a demon its name (Mark 5:1–20), refused to let another demon speak (Mark 1:34), and drove out many spirits with a word (Matt. 8:16). The variety of ways for ministering to the demonized in Scripture point us once more to the need for discernment and listening to the Spirit of God." (Lawrence, 2011)

Whether healing from sickness and disease or casting out demons, listen to the Spirit of God and do what He tells you to do!

DARE TO BELIEVE

After Jesus returned from across the lake, a huge crowd of people quickly gathered around him on the shoreline. Just then, a man saw that it was Jesus, so he pushed through the crowd and threw himself down at his feet. His name was Jairus, a Jewish official who was in charge of the synagogue. He pleaded with Jesus, saying over and over, "Please come with me! My little daughter is at the point of death, and she's only twelve years old! Come and lay your hands on her and heal her and she will live!"

Jesus went with him, and the huge crowd followed, pressing in on him from all sides.

Now, in the crowd that day was a woman who had suffered horribly from continual bleeding for twelve years. She had endured a great deal under the care of various doctors, yet in spite of spending all she had on their treatments, she was not getting better, but worse. When she heard about Jesus's healing power, she pushed through the crowd and came up from behind him and touched his prayer shawl. For she kept saying to herself, "If only I could touch his clothes, I know I will be healed." As soon as her hand touched him, her bleeding immediately stopped! She knew it, for she could feel her body instantly being healed of her disease!

Jesus knew at once that someone had touched him, for he felt the power that always surged around him had passed through him for someone to be healed. He turned and spoke to the crowd, saying, "Who touched my clothes?"

His disciples answered, "What do you mean, who touched you? Look at this huge crowd—they're all pressing up against you." But Jesus's eyes swept across the crowd, looking for the one who had touched him for healing.

When the woman who experienced this miracle realized what had happened to her, she came before him, trembling with fear, and threw herself down at his feet, saying, "I was the one who touched you." And she told him her story of what had just happened.

Then Jesus said to her, "Daughter, because you dared to believe, your faith has healed you. Go with peace in your heart, and be free from your suffering!"

And before he had finished speaking, people arrived from Jairus' house and pushed through the crowd to give Jairus the news: "There's no need to trouble the master any longer—your daughter has died." But Jesus refused to listen to what they were told and said to the Jewish official, "Don't yield to fear. All you need to do is to keep on believing." So they left for his home, but Jesus didn't allow anyone to go with them except Peter and the two brothers, Jacob and John.

When they arrived at the home of the synagogue ruler, they encountered a noisy uproar among the people, for they were all weeping and wailing. Upon entering the home, Jesus said to them, "Why all this grief and weeping? Don't you know the girl is not dead but merely asleep?" Then everyone began to ridicule and make fun of him. But he threw them all outside.

Then he took the child's father and mother and his three disciples and went into the room where the girl was lying. He tenderly clasped the child's hand in his and said to her in Aramaic, "Talitha koum," which means, "Little girl, wake up from the sleep of death." Instantly the twelve-year-old girl sat up, stood to her feet, and started walking around the room! Everyone was overcome with astonishment in seeing this miracle! Jesus had them bring her something to eat. And he repeatedly cautioned them that they were to tell no one about what had happened. (Mark 5:21–43)

Jesus set out to heal Jairus's 12-year-old daughter, but on the way, a woman who had been bleeding for that little girl's entire life reached out and received a healing of her own. There were countless people bumping into Jesus and His disciples along the way, but there is a difference between bumping into Jesus and intentionally reaching out. The woman knew—she knew that she knew that she knew that she knew—that if she could just touch Jesus, healing would be hers. She had faith, and Jesus had the power. So by faith, she touched Him, and she was instantly healed.

Jesus immediately stopped and asked where she was. Not so He could chastise her, or because she had taken the power He needed to heal the little girl (He had more than enough power to heal them both!). No. Jesus called out to her so that He could honor her faith.

Marilyn Hickey writes in her book, *Be Healed*:

> "Since Satan is the exact opposite of all God's goodness, his touch brings sickness, disease, and pain. The woman with the issue of blood was touched by the devil before she was touched by the Lord. Notice that when Jesus spoke to the woman He told her to go in peace. He could have said, 'Be at ease,' and it would have meant the same thing. God's health and blessing brings peace; it puts us at ease. So what does Satan do? He brings dis-ease. Do you realize that when your body is diseased you are out of the peace God intends for you?

> "Satan isn't just your enemy, he is God's enemy. He hates you because he hates God and everything that is like God. When the enemy comes with sickness, it is to harm what God has made in His likeness. The devil wants to destroy everything that God loves and for which He cares; he wants to spoil God's image on the earth. Satan's way of getting back at God is to come against you. Does Satan hate your body? Of course he does. Without a healthy body, you cannot live in the fullness God desires; and without your body, you can no longer live on this earth to rejoice in the Lord and bring glory to His Name.

"Satan knows that every time he hurts you, he hurts the heart of God because God loves you so much. Every parent on earth, who knows the agony of seeing their children sick, has some idea of how God, our heavenly Parent, must feel when we are dis-eased. Most parents would willingly take the illness of their children upon themselves rather than have their offspring ill. This is exactly what the Father did for us when Jesus went to the Cross and died for the sickness of sin. The substitutionary death of Jesus, Who was God in the flesh, redeemed us from sin; and in that full redemption was the healing of your body!

"There is no reason for any of us to be confused about who puts sickness on us. [The devil does!] Jesus took our sickness and disease upon Himself at Calvary. The Lord paid a price for your wholeness that cannot be measured; Jesus redeemed you from the curse of the law by becoming a curse for you. (See Galatians 3:13.) There is certainly no reason why God would put sickness on His children when He paid such a price to remove it." (Hickey)

Dis-ease clearly comes from Satan. But ease, peace, and healing come from the Lord! *"The thief comes only to steal and kill and destroy; I have come that they may have life, and have it to the full"* (John 10:10 NIV). Satan attempted to steal the life of a 12-year-old girl. He successfully stole 12 years from the woman with the issue of blood. But Jesus brought life and hope and a future to both. He brought healing and resurrection. Through healing, God's power is known and He is glorified!

MUCH FAITH, MANY HEALINGS

Afterward, Jesus left Capernaum and returned with his disciples to Nazareth, his hometown. On the Sabbath, he went to teach in the synagogue. Everyone who heard his teaching was overwhelmed with astonishment. They said among themselves, "What incredible wisdom has been given to him! Where did he receive such profound insights? And what mighty miracles flow through his hands! Isn't this Mary's son, the carpenter, the brother of Jacob, Joseph, Judah, and Simon? And don't his sisters all live here in Nazareth?" And they took offense at him.

Jesus said to them, "A prophet is treated with honor everywhere except in his own hometown, among his relatives, and in his own house." He was unable to do any great miracle in Nazareth, except to heal a few sick people by laying his hands upon them. He was amazed at the depth of their unbelief!

Then Jesus went out into the different villages and taught the people. (Mark 6:1–6)

His hometown of Nazareth was the only place recorded in the Bible that Jesus was unable to do many miracles. The reason He couldn't heal more people was not because He didn't have the power to heal, but because people didn't have the faith to receive their healing.

Luke shares a similar account to Mark's, with further detail as to how Jesus responded to this hometown rejection:

Jesus said to them, "I suppose you'll quote me the proverb, 'Doctor, go and heal yourself before you try to heal others.' And you'll say, 'Work the miracles here in your hometown that we heard you did in Capernaum.' But let me tell you, no prophet is welcomed or honored in his own hometown.

"Isn't it true that there were many widows in the land of Israel during the days of the prophet Elijah when he locked up the heavens for three and a half years and brought a devastating famine over all the land? But he wasn't sent to any of the widows living in that region. Instead, he was sent to a foreign place, to a widow in Zarephath of Sidon. Or have you not considered that the prophet Elisha healed only Naaman, the Syrian, rather than one of the many Jewish lepers living in the land?" (Luke 4:23–27)

Jesus acknowledged that the people in Nazareth were rejecting Him and the healing power that came with Him by showing a precedent from the Old Testament in which the very same thing occurred.

In 1 Kings 17, Elijah went to Zarephath where a widow cared for his needs and in turn he healed her son. In 2 Kings 5, Elisha healed Naaman, a Syrian, of leprosy. Jesus says both Elijah and Elisha knew people in their hometowns who needed healing—whose children were dying in the famine, who suffered from leprosy—yet God sent them to foreign lands—and Jesus tells us why: *"no prophet is welcomed or honored in his own hometown"* (Luke 4:24).

In Jesus's hometown, where there was little faith, few healings occurred. But the opposite was also true: outside of His hometown, where people believed they could be healed by simply touching the fringe of His robe, great miracles of God took place (see Matthew 14:36).

Randy Clark writes in his book, *Power to Heal*:

"So the principle is this: Wherever there is more faith, more happens. Whenever there is great faith, great things happen. Where there are more people of faith, more things happen in that congregation than in a congregation where there is less faith. It is that simple. Jesus Himself could do no mighty deeds in Nazareth because of the unbelief of the people there (see Mt. 13:58)." (Clark, Power to Heal: Keys to Activating God's Healing Power in Your Life, 2015)

There is no doubt that Jesus has the power and the desire to heal. But people have a role in healing, too. People must have the faith to receive their healing.

There were two things that amazed Jesus: people's faith (see Luke 7:9) and their lack of it (see Mark 6:6); but only one resulted in healing.

DIFFERENT METHODS, SAME RESULT—HEALED!

After this, Jesus left the coastland of Tyre and came through Sidon on his way to Lake Galilee and over into regions of Syria. Some people brought to him a deaf man with a severe speech impediment. They pleaded with Jesus to place his hands on him and heal him.

So Jesus led him away from the crowd to a private spot. Then he stuck his fingers into the man's ears and placed some of his saliva on the man's tongue. Then he gazed into heaven, sighed deeply, and spoke to the man's ears and tongue, "Ethpathakh," which is Aramaic for "Open up, now!"

At once the man's ears opened and he could hear perfectly, and his tongue was untied and he began to speak normally. Jesus ordered everyone to keep this miracle a secret, but the more he told them not to, the more the news spread! The people were absolutely beside themselves and astonished beyond measure. And they began to declare, "Everything he does is wonderful! He even makes the deaf hear and the mute speak!" (Mark 7:31–37)

Mark 7 records a unique method of healing—spit! A man who is both deaf and mute was brought to Jesus for healing. Jesus placed His fingers in the man's ears, and spit on the man's tongue. Jesus commanded them to *"open"* and immediately the man could speak and hear. *"The people were absolutely beside themselves..."* (v. 37); no one had ever seen anything like it!

While the people seemed excited—*"astonished beyond measure"*—by this unusual healing, Pastor Bill Johnson believes that we can get caught up in patterns and routines. We see success through one method and get locked in to that being the one and only way that God works. Johnson encourages us to stay open to the unique and unprecedented moves of God:

"No two miracles of Jesus recorded in Scripture were done in exactly the same way. I cannot help but wonder if our tendency to get locked into patterns and principles, though they have value, might work against our need to stay connected to what the Father is doing. It is no longer a question of whether it is God's will to heal. Now it is only a question of how.

"Developing an ear for His voice seems to be at the heart of this issue, for faith comes by hearing, not having heard (see Romans 10:17). Faith implies a present-tense relationship with God. What we know can keep us from what we need to know if we do not stay childlike in our approach to life and ministry. **Past success is often what prevents us from greater success**. Our first breakthrough came because we heard from God, but when we create a pattern out of what we last heard, we create a problem ... As Luke 4:4 says, we live by every word that proceeds from God's mouth." (Johnson, 2011)

Wow! Allowing a successful healing to create a pattern in our understanding can actually stop us from seeing another healing.

Johnson continues: "The key for Jesus was not putting mud in a man's eye or telling him to wash in the pool of Siloam (see John 9:6–7). It was not the action done. It was hearing the voice of the Father and doing what He said that made that particular act powerful."

Jesus was constantly using new methods of healing because He was doing what the Father was doing and what the Father was telling Him to do (see John 5:19). And He, because He faithfully followed what God told Him to do, saw success.

On one occasion, God told Him to spit on the man's tongue. On another, He told him to spit in the dirt and make mud. When three men lowered their friend from the roof down to Jesus, God told Him to forgive the man's sins first. One man was told to pick up his mat. Another was told to dip seven times in the river. And each time, when both the Healer and the one being healed obeyed the instructions, healing occurred.

Johnson writes, "Making room for God to do as He pleases and then cooperating with Him is the greatest thing we can do to see an increase in signs and wonders."

God continues to speak today through words of knowledge. When one is in tune with those words, and in tune with the Spirit, and then does what the words and the Spirit say, just stand back and watch God work!

Pastor Johnson affirms, "God has already decided to heal people, and He demonstrated that choice by purchasing the miracle with the stripes on Jesus's body." (Johnson, 2011) If you aren't seeing healing, it isn't because God doesn't want to see you healthy and whole. Perhaps it is because God wants to move in a way that has never been seen before.

DAY 18

SECOND TIME'S A CHARM

When they arrived at Bethsaida, some people brought a blind man to Jesus, begging him to touch him and heal him. So Jesus led him, as his sighted guide, outside the village. He placed his saliva on the man's eyes and covered them with his hands. Then he asked him, "Now do you see anything?"

"Yes," he said. "My sight is coming back! I'm beginning to see people, but they look like trees—walking trees."

Jesus put his hands over the man's eyes a second time and made him look up. The man opened his eyes wide and he could see everything perfectly. His eyesight was completely restored! Then Jesus sent him home with these instructions: "Go home, but don't tell anyone what happened, not even the people of your own village." (Mark 8:22–26)

In the litany of healing miracles that Jesus was anointed by the Holy Spirit to perform while He walked this earth was the *"recovery of sight for the blind"* (Luke 4:18 NIV). In fact, when John the Baptist sends messengers from prison to Jesus to confirm that He is the Messiah, Jesus's *"proof"* of His divinity is that *"the blind are now seeing"* (Luke 7:22). So, for people to bring a blind man to Jesus to be healed, as we read about in Mark chapter 8, is commonplace. And for Jesus to be able to heal the blind man is to be expected. But, of all the blind who were healed while Jesus walked this earth, this one stands out for a very unique reason—this is the only instance in which we see Jesus have to make a second attempt in order to achieve total healing.

Randy Clark writes in *The Essential Guide to Healing*:

"I thank God this instance is recorded in the Bible, for it shows how Jesus ministered when healing did not happen the first time. What did He do? Assume healing must not be the Father's will? No. Did He figure that in the sovereignty of God the man would not be healed? No. After interviewing the man and finding out the healing was partial and incomplete, Jesus simply ministered again. This time the healing was complete.

"This passage shows us some things. First, it is good to stop and re-interview after our initial time of ministry. Second, if the healing is only partial, we should continue ministering. I have seen many people pray for someone's healing and never ask if the person is better. Perhaps they are afraid that the person might not be healed, and then they would not know what to do next. Some people believe it would be wrong to pray a second time because it would show a lack of faith the first time. But we see Jesus doing this very thing—ministering a second time when the first time did not bring the desired result." (Johnson, 2011)

When the people brought the blind man to Jesus, they begged Jesus to *"touch him,"* knowing that a simple touch from Jesus could bring healing. Instead, Jesus offered the man His elbow and led him out of the village. Once He was away from the crowds, Jesus spit in the man's face and covered the unseeing eyes with His hands. Then He asked the man, *"Now do you see anything?"* (v. 23.) The man was thrilled. *"'Yes!' he said. 'My sight is coming back! I'm beginning to see people ...'"* After seeing nothing, he couldn't contain his excitement over seeing something; *"... but they look like trees—walking trees."* The man might have been satisfied with blurry vision, but Jesus was not.

In Mark Batterson's book, *The Grave Robber*, he writes:

"Remember the story of Jesus healing the blind man with [saliva]? It's one of the most encouraging miracles in the Gospels because it took two attempts. Even Jesus had to pray more than once! The first prayer resulted in a partial miracle, but Jesus wasn't satisfied with 20/80 or

20/40 vision. So He doubled back and prayed a second time for a 20/20 miracle: *'Then Jesus laid his hands on his eyes again'* (v. 25 ESV). The operative word is *'again.'* What do you need to pray for again? And again and again and again?

"Some miracles happen in stages—even healing miracles. If you get partial healing or partial relief, praise God for it. But don't settle for half a miracle! Keep praying for the whole miracle to happen." (Batterson, *The Grave Robber: How Jesus Can Make Your Impossible Possible*, 2014)

Nowhere does Scripture say that God wants partial miracles, partial healing, partial peace, partial wholeness, partial forgiveness, or partial ANYTHING for the believer. He wants TOTAL healing, TOTAL peace, TOTAL wholeness, TOTAL forgiveness, and TOTAL fullness of life for His children. As Batterson writes, "When you are receiving your miracle, don't be satisfied with a partial answer." And as Clark attests, praying again does not indicate a lack of faith. In fact, if all you get is part and parcel of God's promises for your life, it can only mean one thing—God's not done yet! Keep praying. Keep believing. Keep praising. Keep receiving until the WHOLE miracle has happened, because TOTAL healing—complete health—is God's will for everyone.

HE IS ALWAYS WILLING, ABLE, AND READY TO HEAL

Now when they came down the mountain to the other nine disciples, they noticed a large crowd of people gathered around them, with the religious scholars arguing with them. The crowd was astonished to see Jesus himself walking toward them, so they immediately ran to welcome him.

"What are you arguing about with the religious scholars?" he asked them.

A man spoke up out of the crowd. "Teacher," he said, "I have a son possessed by a demon that makes him mute. I brought him here to you, Jesus. Whenever the demon takes control of him, it knocks him down, and he foams at the mouth and gnashes his teeth, and his body becomes stiff as a board. I brought him to your disciples, hoping they could deliver him, but they were not strong enough."

Jesus said to the crowd, "Why are you such a faithless people? How much longer must I remain with you and put up with your unbelief? Now, bring the boy to me."

So they brought him to Jesus. As soon as the demon saw him, it threw the boy into convulsions. He fell to the ground, rolling around and foaming at the mouth. Jesus turned to the father and asked, "How long has your son been tormented like this?"

"Since childhood," he replied. "It tries over and over to kill him by throwing him into fire or water. But please, if you're able to do something, anything—have compassion on us and help us!"

Jesus said to him, "What do you mean 'if'? If you are able to believe, all things are possible to the believer."

When he heard this, the boy's father cried out with tears, saying, "I do believe, Lord; help my little faith!"

Now when Jesus saw that the crowd was quickly growing larger, he commanded the demon, saying, "Deaf and mute spirit, I command you to come out of him and never enter him again!"

The demon shrieked and threw the boy into terrible seizures and finally came out of him! As the boy lay there, looking like a corpse, everyone thought he was dead. But Jesus stooped down, gently took his hand, and raised him up to his feet, and he stood there completely set free!

Afterwards, when Jesus arrived at the house, his disciples asked him in private, "Why couldn't we cast out the demon?"

He answered them, "This type of powerful spirit can only be cast out by fasting and prayer." (Mark 9:14–29)

Jesus has just come down off the mount of transfiguration. He is glowing, having met with Elijah and Moses, only to discover that His disciples have failed to do what He has commissioned them to do—heal and cast out demons.

Bill Johnson writes in his book, *The Essential Guide to Healing*:

"When the disciples did not get a supernatural breakthrough as they were accustomed to, they asked Jesus why (see Mark 9:28). He explained that sometimes we need to add fasting and prayer to our pursuit. In other words, some realms in God will not be brought to us—they must be pursued. Whenever we create a theology around what did not happen, we always fall short of God's plan. His intentions are beyond the reach of both our prayer life and our imagination (see Ephesians 3:20)." (Johnson, 2011)

Johnson points out that, when the disciples failed to cast the demon out, the father assumed that the demon was too strong. In the same vein, when people don't see healing today, they create a theology that says we aren't supposed to have everything here on earth, that we have to wait until heaven. But Jesus never said that. Jesus never said that this little boy would have to live with his demon forever.

Johnson continues:

"While it can truthfully be said that Jesus did not heal everyone alive in His day, it must also be noted that He healed everyone who came to Him. No exceptions. The measures of faith people expressed varied, from *'if you are able,'* to *'if you are willing,'* to *'just touch us,'* to *'let me touch you'* to finally *'just say the word'* (see Mark 9:22; Mark 1:40; Matthew 9:29; Mark 6:56; Matthew 8:8). Jesus responded to great faith and little faith. The father who said *'if you are able'* hardly registers on faith's Richter scale, yet his faith was enough to bring Jesus the Healer to the forefront once again. He healed that father's child.

"A major change in theology has taken place over the past two thousand years. When Jesus walked the earth, all sickness was from the devil. Today a large part of the body of Christ believes God either sends sickness or allows it to make us better people by building character and teaching us the value of suffering. If God allows sickness, can we still call the devil a thief? After all, if the thief has permission to steal, it is no longer called stealing. Yet Acts 10:38 tells us *'God anointed Jesus of Nazareth with the Holy Spirit and with power, who went about doing good and healing all who were oppressed by the devil, for God was with Him'* (NKJV).

"This same group who believes God sends sickness also considers those who pray for the sick to be deceived by the devil, or at least be 'out of balance.' Somewhere in today's theology, God took over the devil's job! The early Church knew that the devil came to steal, kill, and destroy, but now the Church gives God the blame. If God truly sent sickness, we would interfere with His great plan by going to a doctor. Of course, this is nonsense. But this change in theology has had its influence in much of the Church. And as we do with any other sin, we need to confess and repent of it. Repentance means to change the way we think. Sorrow over such a sin of misrepresenting God to others must bring about a change in how we view reality. Renewing our minds through repentance will go a long way in getting out of this hole of unbelief and deception. Remember, healing is not just something God does. It is who He is. His name is *Jehovah Rapha*, "The God Who Heals" (see Exodus 15:26). To deny this is to deny the nature of God, who never changes.

"Jesus healed all disease. He accurately and properly represented the Father by demonstrating His love through power. If we have money but turn our backs on the cry of the poor, people have reason to question our walk with God. But if we have the Spirit of the resurrected Christ living in us and turn our backs on the cry of the sick, are we any less guilty? I think not.

"Jesus started His ministry with a statement that would completely define our lives: *'Repent, for the kingdom of heaven is at hand'* (Matthew 4:17). In other words, change the way you think, for I brought My world with Me. And unless you change your perspective on life, you can live within reach of all that you long for, but never taste of its reality." (Johnson, 2011)

One needn't look further than the Scriptures to see that God's will is ALWAYS to heal, restore, and see His children walking in abundant life.

BECAUSE JESUS SAID SO

When Jesus and his disciples had passed through Jericho, a large crowd joined them. Upon leaving the village, they met a blind beggar sitting on the side of the road named Timai, the son of Timai. When he heard that Jesus from Nazareth was passing by, he began to shout "Jesus, son of David, have mercy on me now in my affliction. Heal me!"

Those in the crowd were indignant and scolded him for making so much of a disturbance, but he kept shouting with all his might, "Son of David, have mercy on me now and heal me!"

Jesus stopped and said, "Call him to come to me." So they went to the blind man and said, "Have courage! Get up! Jesus is calling for you!" So he threw off his beggars' cloak, jumped up, and made his way to Jesus. Jesus said to him, "What do you want me to do for you?"

The man replied, "My Master, please, let me see again!"

Jesus responded, "Your faith heals you. Go in peace, with your sight restored." All at once, the man's eyes opened and he could see again, and he began at once to follow Jesus, walking down the road with him. (Mark 10:46–52)

The son of Timai, also referred to in some Bible translations as "blind Bartimaeus," had heard the rumors about Jesus. Not just the rumors about this man's supernatural ability to heal, but also the rumors that He was the Son of God. *"Jesus, son of David"* (v.48), the blind man shouted. In other words, "I know who You are. You are the Messiah. Anointed to bring good news, and recovery of sight to the blind. Jesus, son of David, have mercy on me. Have mercy on me. Show me compassion in my affliction. Heal me!"

The blind man clearly had the faith to cry out to Jesus. But what was it that sent him over the edge, from the faith to cry out to the faith to jump to his feet and run to Jesus?

Randy Clark explains in *The Essential Guide to Healing*:

> "In Mark 10, blind Bartimaeus desperately cried out for Jesus to have mercy on him. Stopping, Jesus said, 'Call him.' So the disciples told Bartimaeus, 'Cheer up! On your feet! He's calling you' (verse 49, NIV).

> "This gave Bartimaeus great faith, which he indicated by throwing his cloak to the ground (verse 50). This cloak was like his social security disability card. It was given by the religious establishment to indicate he was a legitimate beggar, not a scam artist. In his heart, he knew he would not need it anymore. What caused this kind of faith? Hearing the words, 'He's calling you!'

> "That is a word of knowledge. Jesus, through His disciples, shares who and what He wants to heal. [When I am ministering,] I often pick out someone on the first row and ask them, 'How would you feel if Jesus appeared, stood in front of you and said, 'I want to heal you tonight'? Would you be excited? Why? Would you be certain you would be healed? Why?'

> "They usually say, 'Because Jesus said so.' That generates excitement. People are certain they would be healed if Jesus told them He wanted to heal them. That is exactly what He does in a word of knowledge. When people truly understand the purpose of such words and are the benefactors of one (meaning they are the one about whom the word is given), it creates an excitement and a confidence that they will indeed be healed—because Jesus said so through the word of knowledge." (Johnson, 2011)

God has *already* decided to heal you. You can be certain of that. He is calling you to come to Him. Listen for His voice. Listen for His call. As the Word encourages us to do, "*Have courage! Get up! Jesus is calling for you!"* (Mark 10:50). Throw off your "beggar's cloak"—whatever your source of security is that keeps you from receiving total healing—get up, and run to Him.

DAY 21

JESUS, THE OVERCOMER

Before dawn that morning, all the ruling priests, elders, religious scholars, and the entire Jewish council set in motion their plan against Jesus. They bound him in chains, took him away, and handed him over to Pilate.

As Jesus stood in front of the Roman governor, Pilate asked him, "So, are you really the king of the Jews?"

Jesus answered, "You have just spoken it."

Then the ruling priests, over and over, made bitter accusations against him, but he remained silent.

So Pilate questioned him again. "Have you nothing to say? Don't you hear these many allegations they're making against you?" But Jesus offered no defense to any of the charges, much to the great astonishment of Pilate.

Every year at Passover, it was the custom of the governor to pardon a prisoner and release him to the people—anyone they wanted. Now, Pilate was holding in custody a notorious criminal named Barabbas, one of the assassins who had committed murder in an uprising. The crowds gathered in front of Pilate's judgment bench and asked him to release a prisoner to them, as was his custom.

So he asked them, "Do you want me to release to you today the king of the Jews?" (Pilate was fully aware that the religious leaders had handed Jesus over to him because of sheer spite and envy.)

But the ruling priests stirred up the crowd to incite them to ask for Barabbas instead.

So Pilate asked them, "Then what do you want me to do with this one you call the king of the Jews?"

They all shouted back, "Crucify him!"

"Why?" Pilate asked. "What evil thing has he done wrong?" But they kept shouting out with an deafening roar, "Crucify him at once!"

Because he wanted to please the people, Pilate released Barabbas to them. After he had Jesus severely beaten with a whip made of leather straps and embedded with metal, he sentenced him to be crucified.

The soldiers took Jesus into the headquarters of the governor's compound and summoned a military unit of nearly six hundred men. They placed a purple robe on him to make fun of him. Then they braided a victor's crown, a wreath made of thorns, and set it on his head. And with a mock salute they repeatedly cried out, "Hail, your majesty, king of the Jews!" They kept on spitting in his face and hit him repeatedly on his head with a reed staff, driving the crown of thorns deep into his brow. They knelt down before him in mockery, pretending to pay him homage. When they finished ridiculing him, they took off the purple robe, put his own clothes back on him, and led him away to be crucified.

As they came out of the city, they stopped an African man named Simon, a native of Libya. He was passing by, just coming in from the countryside with his two sons, Alexander and Rufus, and the soldiers forced him to carry the heavy crossbeam for Jesus. They brought Jesus to the execution site called Golgotha, which means "Skull Hill." There they offered him a mild painkiller, a drink of wine mixed with gall, but he refused to drink it.

They nailed his hands and feet to the cross. The soldiers divided his clothing among themselves by rolling dice to see who would win them. It was nine o'clock in the morning when they finally crucified him. Above his head they placed *a sign with the inscription of the charge against him, which read, "This is the King of the Jews."*

Two criminals were also crucified with Jesus, one on each side of him. This fulfilled the Scripture that says:

He was considered to be a criminal.

Those who passed by shook their heads and spitefully ridiculed him, saying, "Aha! You boasted that you could destroy the temple and rebuild it in three days. Why don't you save yourself now? Just come down from the cross!"

Even the ruling priests and the religious scholars joined in the mockery and kept laughing among themselves, saying, "He saved others, but he can't even save himself! Israel's king, is he? Let the 'Messiah,' the 'king of Israel,' pull out the nails and come down from the cross right now. We'll believe it when we see it!" Even the two criminals who were crucified with Jesus began to taunt him, hurling insults on him.

For three hours, beginning at noon, darkness came over the earth. About three o'clock, Jesus shouted with a mighty voice in Aramaic, "Eli, Eli, lama sabachthani?"—that is, "My God, My God, why have you turned your back on me?"

Some who were standing near the cross misunderstood and said, "Listen! He's calling for Elijah." One bystander ran and got a sponge, soaked it with sour wine, then put it on a stick and held it up for Jesus to drink. But the rest said, "Leave him alone! Let's see if Elijah comes to rescue him." Just then Jesus passionately cried out with a loud voice and breathed his last. At that moment the veil in the Holy of Holies was torn in two from the top to the bottom.

When the Roman military officer who was standing right in front of Jesus saw how he died, he said, "There is no doubt this man was the Son of God!

Watching from a distance, away from the crowds, were many of the women who had followed Jesus from Galilee and had cared for him. Among them were Mary Magdalene, Mary the mother of Jacob the younger and Joseph, and Salome. Many other women who had followed him to Jerusalem were there too.

Evening was fast approaching, and it was a preparation day before a Sabbath. So a prominent Jewish leader named Joseph, from the village of Ramah, courageously went to see Pilate and asked to have custody of the body of Jesus. Joseph was a highly regarded member of the Jewish council and a follower of Jesus who had focused his hope on God's kingdom realm. Pilate was amazed to hear that Jesus was already dead, so he summoned the Roman officer, who confirmed it. After it was confirmed, Pilate consented to give the corpse to Joseph.

Joseph purchased a shroud of fine linen and took the body down from the cross. Then he wrapped it in the linen shroud and placed it in a tomb quarried from out of the rock. Then they rolled a large stone over the entrance to seal the tomb. Mary Magdalene and Mary the mother of Joseph were there and saw exactly where they laid the body of Jesus. (Mark 15:1–47)

On the first day of the week, as the Sabbath was ending, Mary Magdalene, Mary the mother of Jacob, and Salome made their way to the tomb. It was very early in the morning as the first streaks of light were beginning to be seen in the sky. They had purchased aromatic embalming spices so that they might anoint his body. And they had been asking one another, "Who can roll away the heavy stone for us from the entrance of the tomb?" But when they arrived, they discovered that the very large stone that had sealed the tomb was already rolled away! And as they stepped into the tomb, they saw a young man sitting on the right, dressed in a long white robe. The women were startled and amazed. But the angel said to them, "Don't be afraid. I know that you're here looking for Jesus of Nazareth, who

*was crucified. He isn't here—he has risen victoriously!
Look! See the place where they laid him. Run and tell his
disciples, even Peter, that he is risen. He has gone ahead
of you into Galilee and you will see him there, just like he
told you."*

*They staggered out of the tomb, awestruck, with their
minds swirling. They ran to tell the disciples, but they were
so afraid and deep in wonder, they said nothing to anyone.*
(Mark 16:1–8)

David Jeremiah writes in his book, *Overcomer*:

"The greatest overcomer of all time is Jesus Christ—who
through death, burial, and resurrection overcame our
greatest enemies—sin, Satan, and death. Jesus overcame
these enemies personally; He overcame them power-
fully; and most importantly, He overcame them perma-
nently. That is the great message of the Resurrection."
(Jeremiah, 2018)

NO TAKE-BACKS WITH GOD

And he said to them, "As you go into all the world, preach openly the wonderful news of the gospel to the entire human race! Whoever believes the good news and is baptized will be saved, and whoever does not believe the good news will be condemned. And these miracle signs will accompany those who believe: They will drive out demons in the power of my name. They will speak in tongues. They will be supernaturally protected from snakes and from drinking anything poisonous. And they will lay hands on the sick and heal them."

After saying these things, Jesus was lifted up into heaven and sat down at the place of honor at the right hand of God! And the apostles went out announcing the good news everywhere, as the Lord himself consistently worked with them, validating the message they preached with miracle-signs that accompanied them! (Mark 16:15–20)

The Great Commission that Jesus imparted to His disciples was to "*preach openly the wonderful news of the gospel to the entire human race*" (v. 15): "*Whoever believes the good news and is baptized will be saved*" (v. 16). "*Miracle signs*" would be the result of that belief (v. 17). What were those signs? The power to "*drive out demons*" and "*speak in tongues*" (v. 17), protection against snakes and poison (v. 18, see also Numbers 21:4–9 and John 3:14–16), and the power to heal (v. 18).

Randy Clark writes in *The Essential Guide to Healing*:

"The primary responsibility of discipleship is to hear the voice of the Spirit, then obey it. As the charismatically gifted people of the New Covenant, we are to continue the works of Jesus—especially in healing and deliverance.

"Through Jesus Christ, Christians would be empowered to do works of righteousness—healing, miracles, signs and wonders—as the fruit Jesus spoke of in John 15:8 when He said, 'This is to my Father's glory, that you bear much fruit, showing yourselves to be my disciples.'" (Johnson, 2011)

The proof of discipleship—being a believer—is in the miracle signs. The miracle signs are the fruit that our lives bear from being connected to Jesus, the vine. Clark continues:

"This passage indicates that people who become Christians should be taught to do what Jesus taught the disciples to do. Healing the sick and casting out demons top the list, and nothing indicates that those were only meant to be done until the Bible was canonized. As long as we baptize in the name of the Father, the Son, and the Holy Spirit, we are to continue teaching the newly baptized to heal the sick and cast out demons." (Johnson, 2011)

We must be careful, however, in how we teach others, so that we are teaching them biblically and not based on an evolving theology of the Church. For example, in Jesus's Commission, He does not tell the disciples to pray for the sick, therefore, neither should we teach people to pray for the sick. Clark explains:

"Jesus did not say pray for the sick, He said to heal the sick. When you read the gospels' stories about healings, notice that Jesus and His disciples never prayed petitionary prayers for healing. Instead, they commanded in prayer every time. Their prayer commands were not directed toward God, but toward people's conditions." (Johnson, 2011)

Jesus commanded evil spirits to come out. He commanded curses to be broken. He commanded people to get up and walk. He did not, however, command God to heal someone or pray for God to heal, saying, "if it be Your will." Clark adds:

"Remember, no one in the Bible ever prayed for healing with the words, "If it be Your will." Neither do we see modeled anywhere in the New Testament someone praying for healing using petitionary prayers rather than commands. We should not beg God for healings, remind Him of the person's merit (as if that would move Him more than what His Own Son did to merit the person's healing), or pray long, flowing prayers void of coming to the point of command. Remember, you are not commanding God to do what you say. You are commanding the body to respond because you are an ambassador—a representative of God's Kingdom with authority and power to heal the sick and cast out evil spirits." (Johnson, 2011)

Throughout the Gospels, people were amazed that Jesus spoke with authority. But that same authority is bestowed upon believers— the power and authority to preach, to heal, to cast out. Therefore, we do not have to ask God to heal. Clark explains, "He has delegated authority for that to His disciples."

That authority is a gift to us from the Father, and as Romans 11:29 says: *"And when God chooses someone and graciously imparts gifts to him, they are never rescinded."* There are no take-backs with God. So be bold and obedient. Preaching, healing, and deliverance are expected of you.

HEALING IS YOURS

During the reign of King Herod the Great over Judea, there was a Jewish priest named Zechariah who served in the temple as part of the priestly order of Abijah. His wife, Elizabeth, was also from a family of priests, being a direct descendant of Aaron. They were both lovers of God, living virtuously and following the commandments of the Lord fully. But they were childless since Elizabeth was barren, and now they both were quite old.

One day, while Zechariah's priestly order was on duty and he was serving as priest, it happened by the casting of lots (according to the custom of the priesthood) that the honor fell upon Zechariah to enter into the Holy Place and burn incense before the Lord. A large crowd of worshipers had gathered to pray outside the temple at the hour when incense was being offered. All at once an angel of the Lord appeared to him, standing just to the right of the altar of incense.

Zechariah was startled and overwhelmed with fear. But the angel reassured him, saying, "Don't be afraid, Zechariah! God is showing grace to you. For I have come to tell you that your prayer for a child has been answered. Your wife, Elizabeth, will bear you a son and you are to name him John. His birth will bring you much joy and gladness. Many will rejoice because of him. He will be one of the great ones in the sight of God. He will drink no wine or strong drink, but he will be filled with the Holy Spirit even while still in his mother's womb. And he will persuade many in Israel to convert and turn back to the Lord their God. He will go before the Lord as a forerunner, with the same power and anointing as Elijah the prophet. He will be instrumental in turning the hearts of the fathers in tenderness back to their children and the hearts of the disobedient back to the wisdom of their righteous fathers. And he will prepare a united people who are ready for the Lord's appearing."

Zechariah asked the angel, "How do you expect me to believe this? I'm an old man and my wife is too old to give me a child. What sign can you give me to prove this will happen?"

Then the angel said, "I am Gabriel. I stand beside God himself. He has sent me to announce to you this good news. But now, since you did not believe my words, you will be stricken silent and unable to speak until the day my words have been fulfilled at their appointed time and a child is born to you. That will be your sign!"

Meanwhile, the crowds outside kept expecting him to come out. They were amazed over Zechariah's delay, wondering what could have happened inside the sanctuary. When he finally did come out, he tried to talk, but he couldn't speak a word, and they realized from his gestures that he had seen a vision while in the Holy Place. He remained mute as he finished his days of priestly ministry in the temple and then went back to his own home. Soon afterward his wife, Elizabeth, became pregnant and went into seclusion for the next five months. She said with joy, "See how kind it is of God to gaze upon me and take away the disgrace of my barrenness!" (Luke 1:5–25)

When Elizabeth's pregnancy was full term, she gave birth to a son. All her family, friends, and neighbors heard about it, and they too were overjoyed, for they realized that the Lord had showered such wonderful mercy upon her.

When the baby was eight days old, according to their custom, all the family and friends came together for the circumcision ceremony. Everyone was convinced that the parents would name the baby Zechariah, after his father. But Elizabeth spoke up and said, "No, he has to be named John!"

"What?" they exclaimed. "No one in your family line has that name!"

So they gestured to the baby's father to ask what to name the child. After motioning for a writing tablet, in amazement of all, he wrote, "His name is John."

Instantly Zechariah could speak again. And his first words were praises to the Lord.

The fear of God then fell on the people of their village, and the news of this astounding event traveled throughout the hill country of Judea. Everyone was in awe over it! All who heard this news were astonished and wondered, "If a miracle brought his birth, what on earth will this child become? Clearly, God's presence is upon this child in a powerful way!" (Luke 1:57–66)

Zechariah was about to have a once-in-a-lifetime opportunity—as a priest, the lot had fallen to him to go into the temple of the Lord and burn incense. But that wasn't the only once-in-a-lifetime that God had up His sleeve that day. God had waited for precisely that moment to announce to Zechariah that he would have a son.

Zechariah and his wife Elizabeth were Spirit-filled believers, but had dealt with an affliction for the entirety of their marriage: Elizabeth was barren and unable to have children. Any hope that God would heal them of this affliction had long since passed. They were now well past childbearing years and long past praying for an heir.

Does this story sound familiar? In Genesis 18, we read the story of Abraham and Sarah—Sarah who laughed and Abraham who was 100 years old when their son Isaac was born.

In this instance, no one laughs, but Zechariah did doubt. He asked for proof. His mind was more conformed to the world than to God's miraculous ways (see Romans 12:2). And he was struck mute.

Elizabeth's healing took place first. She became pregnant by her husband. But Zechariah had to wait until his son was born to be healed of his frozen tongue. Immediately upon his mouth opening, Zechariah unleashed the torrent of praises that had been building up in his heart for the past nine months ... maybe even the past 90 years!

Pastor John Kilpatrick teaches that, "Worship flows from those who are blessed." (Kilpatrick, "Door to Blessings")

Zechariah knew there was nothing he had done to deserve being chosen as the father of the one who would prepare the way for the coming Messiah, and that recognition of the undeserved favor of God caused him to worship. God's promises had come true in Zechariah's life, just as He said they would. Zechariah had taken those nine months to listen to God, rather than the world, and his mind—his life—was transformed.

Never give up on your miracle. God doesn't quit just because you are 90 or 100 or barren or mute or any other label that the world puts on you. Healing is yours: *"For all the promises of God in Him are Yes, and in Him Amen,"* (2 Corinthians 1:20 NKJV). When you get a hold of how blessed you are, you can't help but worship!

"OF COURSE, I AM WILLING TO HEAL YOU ..."

One day, while Jesus was ministering in a certain city, he came upon a man covered with leprous sores. When the man recognized Jesus, he fell on his face at Jesus's feet and begged to be healed, saying, "If you are only willing, you could completely heal me."

Jesus reached out and touched him and said, "Of course I am willing to heal you, and now you will be healed." Instantly the leprous sores were healed and his skin became smooth.

Jesus said, "Tell no one what has happened, but go to the priest and show him you've been healed. And to show that you are purified, make an offering for your cleansing, just as Moses commanded. You will become a living testimony to them!"

After this miracle the news about Jesus spread even farther. Massive crowds continually gathered to hear him speak and to be healed from their illnesses. But Jesus often slipped away from them and went into the wilderness to pray. (Luke 5:12–16)

Jesus's reputation preceded Him. He was known as a Healer. And yet the man in Luke 5 *"begged to be healed."*

Why did he have to beg someone whose very nature was to heal? The man certainly hadn't heard of Jesus denying healing to anyone. Nor had he heard of Jesus failing to heal anyone. If that was the case he would have asked, "if you CAN" heal me, not *"If you are only WILLING"* (v.12). He knew Jesus was able. He just didn't know if He was willing.

Even with Jesus's reputation as Healer, even though He had never turned anyone down or failed to heal, the leprous man still worried that Jesus might not want to be associated with him—someone who was unclean.

But, in the words of Joseph Prince, "Jesus always exceeds our expectations."(Prince J., "Come As You Are and Receive Your Miracle") In the context of this particular passage, Prince specified: "Jesus touched him. He wasn't asked to. He didn't have to. But he did."

The leprous man did not say, "Jesus, if you are only willing, TOUCH me and make me clean." That would not even have crossed his mind. He hadn't been touched since his first sore appeared. He would certainly never be so brazen as to ask Jesus to touch him. Nor would it have crossed his mind that he had to. Jesus regularly healed with words alone: *"get up," "take up your mat," "be healed."* He rebuked demons and healed the centurion's son from a great distance. He clearly did not have to touch the man with leprosy. Which is what makes it so great. He didn't have to; He wanted to. *"Of course I am willing to heal you, and now you will be healed"* (vv. 13–14).

And the most miraculous thing happened. Instead of Jesus becoming unclean by touching the leper, the leper was made clean. He was healed!

We don't have to ask God if He is willing to heal us. It is obviously His will to heal. Joseph Prince says we needn't look further than the Cross:

> "Beloved, the more you focus on what Jesus has done for you at the cross, the more you'll experience His divine health in your body and wholeness in every part of your life."

What exactly happened at the Cross? Prince says:

> "Jesus was the apple of God's eye. He was God's darling Son, His infinite joy and delight.

> "Yet, God gave Jesus up for you. That's how much God loves you.

"Just think about it: If you knew you could save a dying person by giving up something precious to you, would you go as far as to give up your only child whom you dearly love for that person?

"Yet, that is exactly what God did to save you. Jesus, His beloved Son, died on the cross to cleanse you, heal you, and redeem you—spirit, soul, and body! **That is how precious you are to God!**" (Prince J., "Come As You Are and Receive Your Miracle")

You are so precious to God that He gave up His one and only Son (see John 3:16) to cleanse, heal, and redeem you. Prince continues:

"Once you realize how very much God loves Jesus, His darling Son, ask yourself this: If God *willingly* gave Jesus up for me, would He withhold healing from me?

"If God withholds your healing after He has already given you Jesus, then it would mean that your healing is greater or more important than Jesus.

"No my friend, He has *already* given you heaven's best. How will He not also **freely** give you all things, including the healing and wholeness you desire? (see Romans 8:32). (Prince J., "Come As You Are and Receive Your Miracle")

The more you look at what Scripture *actually* says and what God *actually* did, you will see just how ridiculous it is to think that He would be unwilling to heal you.

LOVE, AUTHORITY, POWER, DISCERNMENT, AND FAITH

One day many Jewish religious leaders, known as Pharisees along with many religious scholars came from every village of Galilee, throughout Judea, and even from Jerusalem to hear Jesus teach. And the power of the Lord God surged through him to instantly heal.

Some men came to Jesus, carrying a paraplegic man on a stretcher. They attempted to bring him in past the crowd to set him down in front of Jesus. But because there were so many people crowding the door, they had no way to bring him inside. So they crawled onto the roof, dug their way through the roof tiles, and lowered the man, stretcher and all, into the middle of the crowd, right in front of Jesus.

Seeing the demonstration of their faith, Jesus said to the paraplegic man, "My friend, your sins are forgiven!"

The Jewish religious leaders and the religious scholars whispered objections among themselves. "Who does this man think he is to speak such blasphemy? Only God can forgive sins. Does he think he is God?"

Jesus, knowing their thoughts, said to them, "Why do you argue in your hearts over what I do and think that it is blasphemy for me to say his sins are forgiven? Let me ask you, which is easier to prove: when I say, 'Your sins are forgiven,' or when I say, 'Stand up, carry your stretcher, and walk'?"

Jesus turned to the paraplegic man and said, "To prove to you all that I, the Son of Man, have the lawful authority on

*earth to forgive sins, I say to you now, stand up! Carry your
stretcher and go on home, for you are healed."*

*In an instant, the man rose right before their eyes. He stood,
picked up his stretcher, and went home, giving God all the
glory with every step he took.*

*The people were seized with astonishment and dumb-
founded over what they had just witnessed. And they all
praised God, remarking over and over, "Incredible! What
an unbelievable miracle we've seen today!"* (Luke 5:17–26)

Peter Lawrence wrote in his book, *The Spirit Who Speaks*:

"Most of the different ways the Spirit helps us can be
found in Luke 5:17–26, in which Jesus heals a paralyzed
man, and I have found these five principles to be of great
value: **love**, **authority**, **power**, **discernment**, and **faith**.

"Mark begins his version of this story by saying: '*A few
days later, when Jesus again entered Capernaum, the people heard that he had come home*' (Mark 2:1). It looks
as though this was Jesus's home. Matthew 4:13 says,
'*Leaving Nazareth, [Jesus] went and lived in Capernaum*'
(cf. Matt. 9:1). It seems as if this house that was crowded
out with teachers of the law and Pharisees was Jesus's
cottage by the sea, where His mother and brothers
used to come and stay, and the roof that the four men
smashed up was His own (John 2:12). He'd probably built
it Himself, being practical and good at carpentry.

"After a busy time Jesus came home for a rest, only to
be interrupted by important people who'd come all the
way from Jerusalem to argue with Him. He was in the
middle of a tense time that required His full concentra-
tion when, suddenly, vandals broke into His home. My
reaction in such circumstances would probably have
been unprintable—Jesus's reaction was one of love. If
anyone had felt before this incident that they couldn't
disturb Jesus with their problems because He was too

well known, too tired, or too busy, they would have had to think again. When the poor and the needy turned to Jesus for help, He always met them with love.

"When Christians listen to sick people, spend time with them, pray with them, and lay hands lovingly on them—whatever else happens—they should always feel loved.

"Having suffered a hole in his roof, Jesus then faces an atmosphere of skepticism and antagonism from those who challenge His **authority**. Before He heals the paralytic, Jesus says, '*But that you may know that the Son of Man has authority…*' (Luke 5:24).

"Jesus demonstrates His authority to forgive sins by healing the crippled man, simultaneously proving His authority to heal the sick.

"Luke records that on the occasion when the four men lowered their paralyzed friend through the roof, Jesus not only had God's authority but also His **power** to heal the man: '*And the power of the Lord was present for* [Jesus] *to heal the sick*' (Luke 5:17).

"When the four friends lowered the paralyzed man through the roof, Jesus spoke to him. Luke records it like this: '*When Jesus saw their faith, he said, "Friend, your sins are forgiven"*' (Luke 5:20). This is an amazing statement. A more logical account would have read, 'When Jesus saw their faith, He said, "Get up, take your mat, and go home."'

"Presumably Jesus **discerned** that the man needed to have his sins forgiven before being healed. Maybe he was a bad sinner; maybe people had accused him of being a bad sinner because he was crippled; maybe he had a low self-image and thought he was a bad sinner; maybe Jesus needed to forgive him in order to heal him; maybe Jesus needed to forgive him so that he might know how to keep his healing afterward. Whatever the reason, Jesus discerned the need for forgiveness before He healed him. I suspect this was revealed to Him supernaturally, for they were the first words in the conversation.

"I can find no other instance in the Gospels where Jesus forgave someone's sins before healing the sickness, which suggests the presence of a spiritual problem. Once we have welcomed a sick person with love, received **authority** to pray, and sensed the anointing of the Lord's presence to heal the sick, we too may need spiritual **discernment** as to how to minister.

"Jesus began His ministry to the sick man '*when* [He] *saw their faith*' (Luke 5:20). Faith can be present in the person ministering (Luke 7:11–17, 22:50–51), in the sick person (Mark 5:25–34; Acts 14:8–10), or in some other person or friends (Matt. 8:5–13), but faith in God and His power and willingness to heal through Jesus by His Spirit normally needs to be present for God to supernaturally heal someone.

"How do we come by faith? How did the four friends who lowered the paralytic through the roof receive their faith? The implication in Mark's gospel is that a crowd gathered because of what had happened in Capernaum a few days earlier: '*That evening after sunset the people brought to Jesus all the sick and demon-possessed. The whole town gathered at the door, and Jesus healed many who had various diseases*' (Mark 1:32–34). So the whole town had already seen Jesus heal the sick. At the very least I suspect these four friends had seen Jesus healing people, but sick people did not normally have many able-bodied friends. One wonders if the four had themselves been among the sick whom Jesus healed a few days before and had now decided to bring their friend to Jesus.

"When the paralytic's friends brought him to Jesus, He received them with **love**; Jesus knew in His spirit He had the **authority** to heal the man; He sensed the **power** of the Holy Spirit was present for Him to heal the sick; He **discerned** in the Spirit that He needed to offer the sick man the forgiveness of sins; He recognized the **faith** of those who had come to Him, and told the man to get up and walk. The man obeyed and was healed. I believe that hearing the Spirit speak to us today can help us do what Jesus did." (Lawrence, 2011)

BELIEVE BOLDLY!

After Jesus finished giving revelation to the people on the hillside, he went on to Capernaum. There he found a Roman military captain who had a beloved servant he valued highly, and the servant was sick to the point of death. When the captain heard that Jesus was in the city, he sent some respected Jewish elders to plead with him to come and heal his dying servant. So they came to Jesus and told him, "The Roman captain is a wonderful man. If anyone deserves to have a visit from you, it is him. Won't you please come to his home and heal his servant? For he loves the Jewish people, and he even built our meeting hall for us."

Jesus started off with them, but on his way there, he was stopped by friends of the captain, who gave this message: "Master, don't bother to come to me in person, for I am not good enough for you to enter my home. I'm not worthy enough to even come out to meet one like you. But if you would just release the manifestation of healing right where you are, I know that my young servant will be healed. Unlike you, I am just an ordinary man. Yet I understand the power of authority, and I see that authority operating through you. I have soldiers under me who obey my every command. I also have authorities over me whom I likewise obey. So Master, just speak the word and healing will flow." Jesus marveled at this. He turned around and said to the crowd who had followed him, "Listen, everyone! Never have I found even one among the people of God a man like this who believes so strongly in me." Jesus then spoke the healing word from a distance. When the man's friends returned to the home, they found the servant completely healed and doing fine. (Luke 7:1–10)

Roman officers—also called centurions—were not only Gentiles, but they were known enemies of the Jewish people. However, not even the centurions were immune to the stories of a man named Jesus who went about healing the sick and casting out demons. So when a particular centurion who had a sick servant heard that Jesus was nearby, he appealed to the Jewish leaders to seek out Jesus on his behalf.

Why would the Jewish leaders help the Centurion? Because he was no ordinary centurion. This particular centurion was well-respected by the Israelites, because *"he loves the Jewish people"* (v. 5). So well-respected was he that the elders, in their appeal to Jesus, said: *"If anyone deserves to have a visit from you, it is him"* (v. 4).

Jesus was obviously intrigued by their appeal. If the Jews were asking for healing for a Gentile, it was worth checking out. Jesus set out for the Centurion's home, and was nearly there, when some of the officer's friends blocked His path with a message: *"Master, don't bother to come to me in person, for I am not good enough for you to enter my home. I'm not worthy enough to even come out to meet one like you"* (vv. 6–7).

Why the change of heart? Pastor Mike Bickle says, "In his humility, the Centurion was worried about Jesus defiling himself, either by touching a sick—therefore 'unclean'—servant, or by fraternizing with the 'enemy'." (Bickle, "Jesus's Unique Power and Compassion")

The Centurion hadn't changed his mind about wanting Jesus to heal his servant, just his approach: *"But if you would just release the manifestation of healing right where you are, I know that my young servant will be healed. Unlike you, I am just an ordinary man. Yet I understand the power of authority, and I see that authority operating through you. I have soldiers under me who obey my every command. I also have authorities over me whom I likewise obey. So Master, just speak the word and healing will flow"* (vv. 6–8).

Pastor Mike Bickle says: "He was essentially saying, 'I know you have authority over sickness because you are under the God of Israel.' He may not have understood exactly who Jesus was, but he knew that Jesus operated in God's favor."

Jesus *"marveled"* at the Centurion, and said to the crowd following Him: *"I tell you, I have not found such great faith even in Israel"* (v. 9 NIV).

Why did Jesus consider the Centurion's reaction "great faith"? Bickle says:

> "This man who didn't go to the Synagogue, who wasn't trained in the Jewish Messianic prophecies, but he understood in a way that the Pharisees didn't how God and Jesus operated ... that's remarkable! The reason it was such great faith was because it had such clear insight with so little training or evidence." (Bickle, "Jesus's Unique Power and Compassion")

Jesus was constantly surrounded by a crowd of people who had grown up going to the temple, who knew the Hebrew text, who were well-versed in the law and who had heard the prophecies of a coming Messiah, yet who didn't understand the power of God the Father operating through Jesus the Son in the way that the Centurion did. Without ever being formally taught about faith in a coming Messiah, the Centurion possessed it—he knew that Jesus was no ordinary man (v. 8). And because of that faith, Jesus honored the Centurion's request—He spoke from a distance and the servant was healed (v. 10).

This same story is told in Matthew 8, but he adds an extra lesson from Jesus:

> *"Listen to what I am about to tell you. Multitudes of non-Jewish people will stream from the east and the west, to enter into the banqueting feast with Abraham, Isaac, and Jacob in the heavenly kingdom. But many Israelites, born to be heirs of the kingdom, will be turned away and banished into the darkness where there will be bitter weeping and unbearable anguish."* (Matthew 8:11–12)

This was not an isolated incident. This was not the only Gentile that Jesus would heal. The Centurion was not the only non-Jewish person who would show faith worthy of the Promise. Many Gentiles will come into the Kingdom, Jesus says, and feast at the Resurrection table. And many Israelites will be turned away for their unbelief.

Pastor Mike Bickle teaches:

"Not all of our blessing is related to our faith, but a measure of it is. Some blessing we don't take an active part in. But there is an arena of blessing in your life that, if you believe for it you will experience it, and if you don't believe for it you will go without it." (Bickle, "Jesus's Unique Power and Compassion")

Jesus's compassion to heal is for ALL who believe. Believe BOLDLY!

HE IS COMPASSIONATE TOWARD THOSE WHO GRIEVE

Shortly afterward, Jesus left on a journey for the village of Nain, with a massive crowd of people following him, along with his disciples. As he approached the village, he met a multitude of people in a funeral procession, who were mourning as they carried the body of a young man to the cemetery. The boy was his mother's only son and she was a widow. When the Lord saw the grieving mother, his heart broke for her. With great tenderness he said to her, "Please don't cry." Then he stepped up to the coffin and touched it. When the pallbearers came to a halt, Jesus said to the corpse, "Young man, I say to you, arise and live!"

Immediately, the young man moved, sat up, and spoke to those nearby. Jesus presented the son to his mother, alive! A tremendous sense of holy mystery swept over the crowd as they witnessed this miracle of resurrection. They shouted praises to God, saying, "God himself has visited us to bless his people! A great prophet has appeared among us!"

The news of Jesus and this miracle raced throughout Judea and the entire surrounding region. (Luke 7:11–17)

Jesus was on a mission: spread the word that He had come and that the Kingdom of God was at hand, preach to as many people and nations as He could fit into His short time of ministry, and equip His disciples to carry on that mission. Yet, in the midst of this very busy season of ministry, He noticed people, particularly those who were grieving, who were like sheep without a shepherd, who—unlike the Pharisees—were aware of their lack.

Bill Johnson says that Jesus didn't heal everyone alive, but "He healed everyone who came to Him. No exceptions." (Johnson, 2011) Yet in Luke 7, the grieving mother does not seek out Jesus. She either didn't notice His presence because her head was bowed in grief and her eyes were blurred by tears, or she figured it was too late. Her son—her only son—was inside the coffin being carried by the same friends and neighbors who had once carried the body of her husband to the same cemetery.

She may not have noticed Jesus, but He noticed her. Jesus "*saw the grieving mother*," and "*his heart broke for her*" (v. 13). And He didn't miss a beat. He didn't wait to see if she would come to Him. He didn't ask her questions to test her faith. He didn't worry about who was watching or whether He had enough power left in Him since He'd just healed the Centurion's servant. He couldn't wait. He was too moved with compassion. So He went straight to her and "*with great tenderness he said to her, 'Please don't cry'*" (v. 13).

You can feel His heart breaking for her! But He doesn't succumb to trite phrases. He doesn't say, "I wish there was something I could do," or "We don't always understand God's ways," or "He's with his father and the angels now." No way! Scripture says, "*Then…*" THEN. What did He do THEN? "*Then he stepped up to the coffin and touched it. When the pallbearers came to a halt, Jesus said to the corpse, 'Young man, I say to you, arise and live!' Immediately, the young man moved, sat up, and spoke to those nearby*" (vv. 14–15). Wow! And all because Jesus had compassion on a grieving woman, who was too sick in her grief to ever speak a word to Him.

This is the same compassion that believers are called to today. When we are sensitive to the Spirit, it will lead us to people in need. You will sense when someone is going through something, when someone has a need, when God wants to move in power.

John Wimber writes in his book, *The Way In is the Way On*:

> "The reason the Son of God appeared was to destroy the devil's work (see 1 John 3:8). So we, in doing the Father's will, are to bring the Kingdom to people. When we take care of the poor, pray for the sick and clothe the naked,

we will be sensitive to Father's leading in the midst of these precious people and in His time we will see sight restored to the blind, the lame walk, and the lepers cleansed.

"But remember, these 'signs of the Kingdom' are not for the purpose of showing that the Kingdom is here. They point to the fact that our compassionate King is here! Our Lord is the one who heals and delivers out of compassion. It is not a P.R. program to establish Jesus as King. He is King, and our King is full of compassion! He fed the 5,000 not to provide a sign, but because they were hungry. He healed the sick not to provide a sign, but to relieve their suffering. God's Kingdom comes to the lost and the broken because He is full of mercy and compassion." (Wimber, 2006)

Jesus didn't raise this woman's child from the dead to prove anything. He didn't resurrect the boy because of who was watching. He restored life to a child because He had compassion on a woman who was grieving.

In 2 Corinthians 1, Paul writes:

All praises belong to the God and Father of our Lord Jesus Christ. For he is the Father of tender mercy and the God of endless comfort. He always comes alongside us to comfort us in every suffering so that we can come alongside those who are in any painful trial. We can bring them this same comfort that God has poured out upon us. And just as we experience the abundance of Christ's own sufferings, even more of God's comfort will cascade upon us through our union with Christ. (vv. 3–5)

God is the source of all comfort, and He comforts us so that we can comfort others with the same comfort that we have been comforted by. Comforting, compassionate, merciful, gracious—this is who God is and will always be.

THE REAL QUESTION

John's disciples reported to him in prison about all the wonderful miracles and the works Jesus was doing. So John dispatched two of his disciples to go and inquire of Jesus. When they came before the Master, they asked him, "Are you the coming Messiah we've been expecting, or are we to continue to look for someone else? John the prophet has sent us to you to seek your answer."

Without answering, Jesus turned to the crowd and healed many of their incurable diseases. His miracle power freed many from their suffering. He restored the gift of sight to the blind, and he drove out demonic spirits from those who were tormented.

Only then did Jesus answer the question posed by John's disciples. "Now go back and tell John what you have just seen and heard here today. The blind are now seeing. The crippled are now walking. Those who were lepers are now cured. Those who were deaf are now hearing. Those who were dead are now raised back to life. The poor and broken are given the hope of salvation. And tell John these words: 'The blessing of heaven comes upon those who never lose their faith in me no matter what happens.'"

After John's messengers departed, Jesus spoke about John to the audience crowded around him, saying, "What kind of man did you expect to see out in the wilderness? Did you expect to see a man who would be easily influenced and shaken by the shifting opinions of others? Who did you really go there to see? Did you expect to see a man decked out in the splendid fashion of the day? They are the ones who live in the lap of luxury, embracing the values of this world. Or did you discover a true prophet out in the lonely wilderness? Yes, John was a legitimate prophet. Even more than that, he was the fulfillment of this Scripture:

'See, I am sending my prophetic messenger who will go ahead of me and prepare hearts to receive me.'

"Throughout history there was never found a man as great as John the Baptizer. Yet those who now walk in God's kingdom realm, though they appear to be insignificant, will become even greater than he."

When the common and disreputable people among the audience heard Jesus say this, they acknowledged that it was the truth, for they had already experienced John's baptism. But the hearts of the Jewish religious leaders and experts of the law had rejected the clear purpose of God by refusing to be baptized by John.

Jesus continued, saying, "How could I describe the people of this generation? Can't you see? You're like children playing games on the playground, complaining to friends, 'You don't like it when we want to play Wedding. And you don't like it when we want to play Funeral. Why will you neither dance nor mourn?'

"When the prophet John came fasting and refused to drink wine, you said, 'He's crazy! There's a demon in him.' Yet when the Son of Man came and went to feasts and drank wine, you said, 'Look at this man! He is nothing but a glutton and a drunkard. He spends all his time with tax collectors and other notorious sinners.'

"Nevertheless, I say to you, the wisdom of God will be proven true by the expressions of godliness in everyone who follows me." (Luke 7:18–35)

John the Baptist began his ministry before Jesus did, and so, as John went about proclaiming the coming Kingdom and baptizing, he gathered many followers. After John baptized Jesus, Jesus began gaining followers too. Some left John and followed Jesus, but others were reluctant to leave John. John tried to make it clear to his followers that he wanted them to follow Jesus, but many just kept hanging around. In verse 18, we see John's followers visiting him in prison, reporting to him about the miracles that Jesus was doing. John saw an opportunity here and sent his disciples to ask Jesus: *"Are you the coming Messiah we've been expecting, or are we to continue to look for someone else?"* (v. 20).

Did John suddenly become a doubter now that he was in prison and couldn't see Jesus for himself? Pastor Mike Bickle doesn't think so:

> "I believe John sent them for the sake of the disciples, not because John was wavering. I believe the disciples of John need the answer—not John himself ... John's not confused. He saw the Spirit come on Jesus. He heard the audible voice of the Father: 'This is My Son'."
> (Bickle, "Jesus's Unique Power and Compassion")

John wanted his disciples to become followers of Jesus, fully committed to Christ, so he sent them on a mission to see for themselves. Bickle says, "Jesus knew what John was up to." Why does he say that? Because as soon as John's disciples ask Jesus if He is for real, *"Without answering, Jesus turned to the crowd and healed many of their incurable diseases. His miracle power freed many from their suffering. He restored the gift of sight to the blind, and he drove out demonic spirits from those who were tormented"* (v. 21).

"Are you the One?" the disciples asked. And Jesus proved it by fulfilling the prophecies of Isaiah. Bickle says, "Every Jewish boy knew the prophecies of Isaiah 35." Thus, when the disciples of John saw Jesus open the eyes of the blind, they knew He was the One.

Jesus tells the men to go back and report to John what they have seen— *"the blind see, the lame walk, the lepers are cleansed, the deaf hear, the dead are raised"* (v. 22 NKJV)—and He adds this extra little beatitude: *"And blessed is he who is not offended because of Me"* (v. 23 NKJV).

Why the addendum? Pastor Mike Bickle says:

> "People are offended at God for two reasons: what God does and what God doesn't do.

> "I believe Jesus knew He was not going to deliver John the Baptist. He was sure He wasn't. And I believe John knew that too, because he knew Jesus was increasing and he was decreasing to the point of phasing out of the picture completely. However, Isaiah 35 says Jesus opens blind eyes and Isaiah 61 says He came to set the captives free, so John's disciples surely thought that since Jesus did the one He would surely do the other and John was going to get set free.

> "This is one of the most important teachings of Jesus in the midst of miracle power. Because when the power of God increases, we bring our natural mindset into the equation, and we assume that bigger is always better, easier is always better, always. But the Lord says, even when I am manifesting my power, there will be times you have to trust my leadership because there will be things I do that are completely the opposite of what you think I should be doing and there will be things I'm not doing that you think I should be because I'm God—like delivering the most righteous man that ever walked this earth." (Bickle, "Jesus's Unique Power and Compassion")

God did not deliver John from prison. Jesus did not raise John from the dead after he'd been beheaded (see Mark 6:14–29). But Jesus didn't want there to be any confusion—He emphasizes that John was great and his faith was unwavering:

> *After John's messengers left, Jesus began to speak to the crowd about John: "What did you go out into the wilderness to see? A reed swayed by the wind? If not, what did you go out to see? A man dressed in fine clothes? No, those who wear expensive clothes and indulge in luxury are in palaces. But what did you go out to see? A prophet? Yes, I tell you, and more than a prophet. This is the one about whom it is written:*

"'I will send my messenger ahead of you, who will prepare your way before you.'

I tell you, among those born of women there is no one greater than John ..." (Luke 7:24–28 NIV).

Pastor Mike Bickle says: "A reed is real weak and fragile. Even a little wind can knock a reed over. Jesus said to the multitude, do you really think John is bending and breaking under the oppression of Herod? You think he's a reed? Then you don't know John." In other words, Jesus was saying, "If you think John sent his disciples here to ask if I was the Messiah because HE doubted, then you don't know John, because he is greater than any man born of a woman. He alone was chosen by God, as a messenger, to prepare the way for the Messiah. He won't compromise his faith. He won't shut up about Jesus to appease Herod. He is the greatest."

AND YET, Jesus adds to His statement about John being the greatest: *"yet the one who is least in the kingdom of God is greater than he"* (v. 28 NIV). He was saying, "John is the greatest, yet the rest of you are greater." How is that possible? Bickle says:

> "John the Baptist was in the old covenant time. John the Baptist was before the Cross. And though John was the greatest of everyone in the old covenant—a born-again believer, after the Resurrection of Jesus and after the day of Pentecost, because God dwells in our spirit—beloved the newest believer has more spiritual privilege than John the Baptist, because we have the indwelling Spirit living in us." (Bickle, "Jesus's Unique Power and Compassion")

As He is speaking to the crowd, Jesus asks the real question, "John isn't wavering, are you?"

WE ARE PARTNERS
WITH CHRIST

*Soon afterward, Jesus began a ministry tour throughout the
country, visiting cities and villages to announce the wonderful news of God's kingdom realm. His twelve disciples
traveled with him and also a number of women who had
been healed of many illnesses under his ministry and set
free from demonic power. Jesus had cast out seven demons
from one woman. Her name was Mary Magdalene, for she
was from the village of Magdala. Among the women were
Susanna and Joanna, the wife of Chusa, who managed
King Herod's household. Many other women who sup-
ported Jesus's ministry from their own personal finances
also traveled with him.* (Luke 8:1–3)

When Jesus ministered throughout the land, He didn't go alone. He
took His twelve disciples with Him, *"and also a number of women
who had been healed of many illnesses under his power and set free
from demonic power"* (v. 2).

Scripture is clear that faith is required to receive healing: *"'My
daughter, be encouraged. Your faith has healed you.' And instantly
she was healed!"* (Matthew 9:22). So obviously these were women
of faith, women who believed that Jesus was Who He said He was,
and who wanted to be part of His mission. They had believed in His
power first, and then personally experienced the manifestation of
that power in their own healing. They had a testimony of healing
and clearly wanted to share it with the world.

Myles Munroe says:

> "One of the great truths of the Bible is that whenever God
> gets ready to do anything in the earth, He always works

through a person or a group of people whom He has called and who have willingly responded to Him. The human factor is key for God's activity on the earth. When God prepared to deliver the Israelites from Egypt, He called Moses. When He got ready to rescue His people from the Midianites, He called Gideon. When God wanted to warn His disobedient people of His judgment and call them back to Him, He called Elijah, Isaiah, Jeremiah, Amos, and the other prophets. When God was ready to send His Son into the world, He chose Mary, a humble peasant girl, to be His mother. When Jesus Christ prepared to send His message of salvation throughout the world, He called and anointed men and women—His Church—and commissioned them for the mission. This illustrates an incredible principle under which God operates: Without God we cannot, and without us God will not. For everything that God desires to do in the earth, He enters into partnership with those to whom He has already given dominion." (Munroe, *The Purpose and Power of Love & Marriage*, 2002)

How powerful! God "enters into partnership" with men and women who can carry out His will on earth, that will being "*to be hope for the poor, freedom for the brokenhearted, and new eyes for the blind, and to preach to prisoners, 'You are set free'!*" (Luke 4:18–19). Healing, freedom, hope.

In the very first book of the Bible, God gives dominion to men and women over the earth (see Genesis 1:26 NKJV). Munroe says:

"God made the world. Then He made men and women and gave them dominion over all the works of His hands. Man was created to be the 'god' of this world. He was given full authority in the earth realm, and God will not supersede that authority. This means that when God said, 'Let them rule ... over all the earth,' He was ordering the dominion of the world in such a way as to make the rule of humans essential for the accomplishment of His purposes. He causes things to happen on earth when men and women are in agreement with His will." (Munroe, The Purpose and Power of Love & Marriage, 2002)

Men and women have dominion, or authority, over the earth; but power comes from aligning with God's will and partnering with Him to see that work accomplished. Munroe says that to enter into that partnership with God we must "willingly respond" to His call. To willingly respond means to say "yes" to both what God is calling you to do AND to who He says you are.

> "I'm washed, I'm forgiven, I'm whole, and I'm healed. I'm cleansed and I'm glory bound. I am only a sojourner on the earth. I am but a pilgrim on this planet, on my way to perfection, and I don't need anybody to tell me who I am, because I know who I am. I am a child of the King, a son (or daughter) of God, born again through Jesus Christ, bought with the price of His blood. I am a new creation, totally new, thoroughly loved and completely accepted as a child of my Father, precious in His sight." (Munroe, *The Purpose and Power of Love & Marriage*, 2002)

When Jesus ministered throughout the land, He took His male and female disciples with Him so that they could learn firsthand to walk in God's will and God's power. And when Jesus ascended to heaven, He sent the Holy Spirit to continue to guide us and lead us to do God's powerful works, in partnership with the One who created us to have dominion here on earth.

DAY 30

BE WITH HIM

Jesus summoned together his twelve apostles and imparted to them authority over every demon and the power to heal every disease. Then he commissioned them to preach God's kingdom realm and to heal the sick to demonstrate that the kingdom had arrived. As he sent them out, he gave them these instructions: "Take nothing extra on your journey. Just go as you are. Don't carry a staff, a backpack, food, money, not even a change of clothes. Whatever home welcomes you as a guest, remain there and make it your base of ministry. And wherever your ministry is rejected and not welcomed, you are to leave that town and shake the dust off your shoes as a testimony before them."

The apostles departed and went into the villages with the wonderful news of God's kingdom realm, and they instantly healed diseases wherever they went. (Luke 9:1–6)

In the first two verses of Luke chapter 9, Jesus gives his twelve newly called apostles three instructions: preach the gospel, heal the sick, and cast out demons. These are the twelve people closest to Jesus in His adult life on earth, called to help Him carry out His work, thus these three instructions were instrumental in fulfilling Jesus's mission.

Pastor Robert Morris teaches:

"We are three parts: spirit, soul, body. In this passage, Jesus is telling his apostles to set people free—completely free—in spirit, soul, and body. 'Preach the Gospel'— so your spirit can be saved and you can live eternally. 'Heal the sick'—refers to your physical body. And 'cast out demons' refers to your soul, because that is where demons torment us—in our mind (thoughts), will, and emotions (feelings). If you want to boil it down, Jesus is saying: help people." (Morris, "My Christian Calling" from the "Why Am I Here" sermon series)

Help people. Free people. In spirit, soul, and body. That is the essence of the Gospel. There is one caveat, however. Morris continues: "This is what Jesus called the disciples to do. But he called them to be something before he called them to do something. The power to do comes from the power to be."

What is Morris talking about? What did Jesus call the disciples to be? The answer is found in Mark 3:14–15: *"He [Jesus] appointed twelve that they might **be with him** and that he might send them out to preach and to have authority to drive out demons"* (NIV, emphasis added).

Did you catch it? Before Jesus gave them something to do—to preach and heal and drive out demons—he appointed them to be—*"be with him."* The Passion Translation says it this way: *"He wanted them to be continually at his side as his friends, and so that he could send them out"* (v. 14). He wanted them with Him, by His side, to accompany Him, as His friends. Friends spend time together, getting to know one another, sharing their hearts and fellowshipping with one another. That's what Jesus wanted from His disciples—He wanted them to spend time with Him and learn His heart. Why? "... *SO THAT HE COULD SEND THEM OUT"* (v. 14.). You wouldn't ask someone to represent you who didn't know you and neither would Jesus. He needed these men to learn His heart and where His power came from before they could go out and operate in that same power.

Pastor Robert Morris says:

> "Before He appointed them to do, He appointed them to be. He said, '*be with Me.*' This was their number one priority as disciples, and it's our number one priority as disciples—to be with Him—because the power to do comes from the power to be. He wanted to give them power to do—power to preach, power to heal, and power to cast out demons. And that power only comes from being connected to Jesus." (Morris, "My Christian Calling" from the "Why Am I Here" sermon series)

Jesus's commission to preach, to heal, and to cast out demons wasn't for the twelve apostles alone. Jesus commissioned the twelve so that they would share the Gospel message with others. And then those others would share it with others. And those others would share it with others and so forth until Jesus's message has literally gone into all the world and disciples have been made in all nations.

Is everyone you know a Christian? No? Then the commission hasn't ended. The call is the same—to preach the gospel, heal the sick, and cast out demons in the name and power of Jesus. With this in mind, according to Pastor Robert: "Our Christian calling is to be Christians—'like Christ'—but we aren't going to be like Christ unless we spend time with Him."

> The council members were astonished as they witnessed the bold courage of Peter and John, especially when they discovered that they were just ordinary men who had never had religious training. Then they began to understand the effect Jesus had on them simply by spending time with him (Acts 4:13)

Be continually at Jesus's side, like a friend, so that others will see in your countenance that you have been with Him. Then, He can send you out!

CHRIST HAS FULFILLED THE LAW

One day there was a crowd gathered around Jesus, and among them was a man who was mute. Jesus drove out of the man the spirit that made him unable to speak. Once the demon left him, the mute man's tongue was loosed and he was able to speak again. The stunned crowd saw it all and marveled in amazement over this miracle!

But there were some in the crowd who protested, saying, "He casts out demons by the power of Satan, the demon king." Others were skeptical and tried to persuade Jesus to perform a spectacular display of power to prove that he was the Messiah.

Jesus, well aware of their every thought, said to them, "Every kingdom that is split against itself is doomed to fail and will eventually collapse. If it is true that Satan casts out his own demons through me, how could his kingdom remain intact? If Satan gives me the power to cast out his demons, who is it that gives your exorcists their power? Let them become your judges! Go and ask them and they will tell you. Yet if I am casting out demons by God's mighty power, God's kingdom realm is now released upon you— but you still reject it!

"Satan's belongings are undisturbed as he stands guard over his fortress kingdom, strong and fully armed with an arsenal of many weapons. But when one stronger than he comes to attack and overpower him, the stronger one will empty the arsenal in which he trusted. The conqueror will ransack his kingdom and distribute all the spoils of victory. This is a war, and whoever is not on my side is against me,

*and whoever does not gather the spoils with me will be for-
ever scattered.*

*"When a demon is cast out of a person, it goes to wander
in the waterless realm, searching for rest. But finding no
place to rest it says, 'I will go back to the body of the one I
left.' When it returns, it finds the person like a house that
has been swept clean and made tidy but is empty. Then it
goes and enlists seven demons more evil than itself, and
they all enter and possess the person, leaving that one with
a much worse fate than before."*

*While he was saying all this, a woman shouted from the
crowd, "God bless the one who gave you birth and nursed
you as a child!"*

*"Yes," said Jesus. "But God will bless all who listen to the
word of God and carefully obey everything they hear."*
(Luke 11:14–28)

The passage above reveals a truth about nature: it has opposing
forces, opposing kingdoms, opposing "rulers." The crowd who witnessed Jesus's miracles—in this case, a demon being dispelled who
had caused a man to be mute—wondered by what authority Jesus
was able to heal: by the authority and power of God, or the authority
and power of the devil?

Pastor Creflo Dollar seeks to help us understand these two
opposing spiritual forces:

"The Law of the Spirit of Life in Christ Jesus encompasses
everything God has promised in His Word—the blessing,
eternal life, faith, a recreated human spirit, peace, pros-
perity, the gifts of the Spirit, healing, deliverance, protection, the Holy Spirit, the fruit of the Spirit, and more.
It is the law that governs the Kingdom of God.

"On the other end of the spectrum is the Law of Sin and
Death, which governs Satan's kingdom, the Kingdom of
Darkness. This law is the reciprocal of the Law of Life

in Christ Jesus and includes fear, the curse, sin, condemnation, bondage, poverty, oppression, and depression, addiction, sickness, physical death, and ultimately, separation from God in Hell. The Law of Sin and Death, when operating in your life, will result in a miserable existence both on earth and after death. It is from this law that Jesus came to redeem every man." (Dollar, *Overcoming Fear: Eliminating the Bondage of Fear*, 2014)

The crowd wondered which spiritual force Jesus bowed to—did He cast out demons by the power of the "*demon king*," or by the power of God as His chosen Messiah? Jesus points out how ridiculous this is. If Satan was casting out his own demons, wouldn't his kingdom then fall? Clearly He was casting out demons by the power of God and releasing God's Kingdom amongst them—if only they would believe.

We too have the power to choose which spiritual force we will bow to—God or the enemy, fear or faith. Dollar says, "Faith allows God in your life while fear is an entry point through which Satan gains access."

Jesus warns His listeners that once a demon is cast out of a person, that person then needs to fill up those empty spaces with the Truth, otherwise the demon will come back stronger than it left (see Luke 11:24–26). The same is true of fear—to overcome fear once and for all, we have to fill up our storehouses with faith.

Dollar says,

"The powerful thing about God's Word is that when you locate a promise of God, you locate the faith it takes to bring it to pass. From the start, you have already been given the advantage where your faith is concerned. Every scripture has faith built into it, which, when deposited in your heart, will pull the unseen spiritual things into the natural realm." (Dollar, *Overcoming Fear: Eliminating the Bondage of Fear*, 2014)

Fear opposes the promises of God, but faith brings them to pass. Don't let the devil find your spirit "*tidy but empty*" (v. 25). Fill yourself up with the Word of God! Study the Word. Believe the Word. Declare the Word. And receive God's promises for your life—promises for good and not for evil, plans for a future and a hope (see Jeremiah 29:11).

> *So now the case is closed. There remains no accusing voice of condemnation against those who are joined in life-union with Jesus, the Anointed One. For the "law" of the Spirit of life flowing through the anointing of Jesus has liberated us from the "law" of sin and death. For God achieved what the law was unable to accomplish, because the law was limited by the weakness of human nature.*

> *Yet God sent us his Son in human form to identify with human weakness. Clothed with humanity, God's Son gave his body to be the sin-offering so that God could once and for all condemn the guilt and power of sin. So now every righteous requirement of the law can be fulfilled through the Anointed One living his life in us. And we are free to live, not according to our flesh, but by the dynamic power of the Holy Spirit!* (Romans 8:1–4)

THOU ART LOOSED

One Sabbath day, while Jesus was teaching in the synagogue, he encountered a seriously handicapped woman. She was crippled and had been doubled over for eighteen years. Her condition was caused by a demonic spirit of bondage that had left her unable to stand up straight. When Jesus saw her condition, he called her over and gently laid his hands on her. Then he said, "Dear woman, you are free. I release you forever from this crippling spirit." Instantly she stood straight and tall and overflowed with glorious praise to God! The Jewish leader who was in charge of the synagogue was infuriated over Jesus healing on the Sabbath day. "Six days you are to work," he shouted angrily to the crowd. "Those are the days you should come here for healing, but not on the seventh day!" The Lord said, "You hopeless frauds! Don't you care for your animals on the Sabbath day, untying your ox or donkey from the stall and leading it away to water? If you do this for your animals, what's wrong with allowing this beloved daughter of Abraham, who has been bound by Satan for eighteen long years, to be untied and set free on a Sabbath day?" When they heard this, his critics were completely humiliated. But the crowds shouted with joy over the glorious things Jesus was doing among them. (Luke 13:10–17)

The Modern English Version of Luke 13 describes the woman in this passage as having a "*spirit of infirmity*":

And there was a woman who had a spirit of infirmity for eighteen years and was bent over and could not straighten herself up. When Jesus saw her, He called her and said to her, "Woman, you are loosed from your infirmity". Then He laid His hands on her, and immediately she was made straight and glorified God (Luke 13:11–13 MEV).

Marilyn Hickey defines the word *infirmity* as:

"Something that causes a person to be 'not firm' or lacking in wholeness. A condition that makes an individual weak or feeble is referred to as an infirmity. Debilitating diseases such as muscular dystrophy or multiple sclerosis can be classified as infirmities. Many wheelchair victims suffer from some sort of infirmity. As some people get older, their bodies lose strength and they become infirm—feeble or tottery. People can become feeble in mind as well as body. Both senility and Alzheimer's disease are infirmities of the mind. The word 'infirm' also means 'to be unstable or irresolute in one's thinking and actions.' ... Infirmities or weaknesses are often inherited. We hear of things such as diabetes or heart disease being passed down from generation to generation." (Hickey)

Infirmity covers a lot of ground, and could be the result of heredity or age or any other type of weakening, but might be summed up as simply as: "not well."

The woman who Jesus encountered on the Sabbath was not well. She was bent over. She couldn't stand up straight from the weight of oppression. She had a demon on her back and she couldn't get him off.

The MEV describes her as having a *"spirit of infirmity"* but The Passion Translation describes her as having a *"spirit of bondage."* Hickey says:

"One day in the synagogue Jesus read Isaiah 61:1–2 and shocked the listeners by saying the prophet's words were fulfilled in Him that day. (See Luke 4:17–21.) Isaiah said the Messiah would '... *proclaim liberty to the captives, and the opening of the prison to them that are bound.*' Later when Jesus healed the woman who had been bent over for 18 years by an '*infirmity,*' He said she had been bound by Satan. This '*daughter of Abraham*' was in bondage to the devil's evil work, but the Lord loosed her body from the imprisonment which had bound her for so long (see Luke 13:11-16). Jesus said sickness holds people in bondage, but He came to set us free.

Jesus freed the woman who was bound by her infirmity. He came to set us free!

Matthew 8:17 says, *"This* [healing and casting out demons] *was to fulfill what was spoken through the prophet Isaiah: 'He took up our infirmities and bore our diseases'"* (NIV). He took them *"up"*—up on the cross—and left them there where they could no longer touch us.

Not every church teaches what the Word of God says. Hickey explains:

> "Unfortunately, many fine Christians have been deceived by denomination doctrine that doesn't agree with the truth of God's Word. How many well-meaning people have you met who are 'suffering for Jesus' because they believe this is pleasing to the Lord? These people think their sickness or unfortunate circumstance has been allowed or even planned by God to humble or mature them. They 'grin and bear it,' but never try to remove it, because they have been told God will reward them according to how patiently they have suffered. This is oppression! No one will ever reach spiritual maturity through the affliction of the flesh." (Hickey)

Jesus suffered for you, so that you wouldn't have to suffer. Jesus bore your sins, because He knew you couldn't. Jesus took up your infirmities, so they could no longer touch you. Do not stay bound by infirmity, weakness, disease, or Satan, when Jesus has already paid the price for you. Healing is yours! Thou art loosed!

IT IS ALWAYS HIS WILL TO HEAL

One day Jesus was on his way to dine with a prominent Jewish religious leader for a Sabbath meal. Everyone was watching him to see if he would heal anyone on the Sabbath. Just then, standing right in front of him was a man suffering with his limbs swollen with fluid.

Jesus asked the experts of the law and the Pharisees who were present, "Is it permitted within the law to heal a man on the Sabbath day? Is it right or wrong?" No one dared to answer. So Jesus turned to the sick man, took hold of him, and released healing to him, then sent him on his way.

Jesus said to them all, "If one of your children or one of your animals fell into a well, wouldn't you do all you could to rescue them even if it was a Sabbath day?"

There was nothing they could say—all were silenced.
(Luke 14:1–6)

John Bevere writes in his book, *Honor's Reward:* "A person with a religious spirit is one who uses My Word to execute his own will!" (Bevere, Honor's Reward: Unlocking the Power of the Forgotten Virtue, 2019)

This can be said of the healing account in Luke 14. "*Everyone was watching*" to see if Jesus would heal on the Sabbath. By this point they clearly knew He could, but would He? Throughout the Gospels we see the religious leaders of the day watching and waiting to trap Jesus based on religious law. What were they trying to prove? They wanted to prove that He wasn't the Messiah, because they believed the Messiah would follow the letter of the law.

In Matthew 5:17, Jesus says: "*If you think I've come to set aside the law of Moses or the writings of the prophets, you're mistaken. I have come to fulfill and bring to perfection all that has been written.*" They think He is breaking the law, but He is actually perfecting it. He came to fulfill the law, not abolish it. And yet it doesn't look like they are expecting it, because—as Bevere says—they are trying to carry out their own will, their own standards for living, their own justice, not God's.

According to the religious leaders, nearly everything Jesus did defied the law (as they defined it): He went around associating with tax collectors and sinful women; He healed on the Sabbath; He even touched the unclean.

In a subsequent story in the book of Luke chapter 17, ten men with leprosy came to Jesus for healing. He seemingly hasn't done anything according to the cultural rules and regulations of the day, so why would anyone expect this time to be different? Surely He would touch them or let them touch His robe, or spit on some mud, or tell them to dip in the Jordan. But this time He told them to follow the rules. He told them to do what was required of someone who was "*unclean*" based on Levitical law (see Leviticus 14)—"*Go to be examined by the Jewish priests*" (Luke 17:14). Without a word, they headed in the direction of the priests. But they never made it—at least one of them didn't—because "*they were healed while walking along the way*" (v. 14). Jesus proves it is God who heals by healing them before they ever arrived to be examined.

Bevere says, "We don't want to merely obey God: we need to catch His heart. It is then we will glimpse the wisdom behind His directives, and not just see them as laws."

The heart of God is to heal. The heart of God is love, not law. Jesus wanted everyone the Father had sent Him to come into the Kingdom with Him (see John 18:9)—Jew and Gentile, clean and unclean, religious leaders and ordinary men and women. And while some came to Him willingly—dropping their nets or turning around and returning as soon as they saw their healing—others had a hard time opening themselves to the upside-down ways of Jesus.

Bevere says:

> "Often God will send us what we need in a package we
> don't want. Why? To let us know He's God and we cannot
> second-guess Him. We cannot search for answers merely
> with our heads; we must seek Him and His provision with
> our hearts. Scripture cannot be interpreted from our lim-
> ited human mental understanding. There must be a breath
> of the Spirit of God. He alone gives wise counsel and cor-
> rect application." (Bevere, *Honor's Reward: Unlocking the
> Power of the Forgotten Virtue*, 2019)

Jesus did not come in the package that many wanted. They wanted
Him to enforce the law of Moses. They wanted Him to be a hand-
some and mighty warrior like David. They wanted Him to justify
the way they had interpreted the Scriptures and the way they were
living them out. They weren't looking for someone who washed feet,
forgave sins (no matter how long the list was), and interpreted the
Scriptures differently than they did. They weren't looking for someone who said, "Actually, you are all wrong. Not one of you has gotten
it exactly right." Some of them stopped listening after that. But for
the ones who had ears to hear and eyes to see and minds to understand—they were "*instantly healed*" (see Matthew 13:15).

Bevere says, "The knowledge of God's Word without love is a
destructive force because it puffs us up with pride and legalism."

This is precisely what Jesus encountered on that Sabbath when
He healed the man with the swollen limbs. He was surrounded by
people who knew what the Scriptures said, but didn't know the love
that undergirded the law. The law was built on love. Everything that
God has ever done has been based on His love for His people. Those
who know His heart, know that it is always—no matter what day it
is—it is always His will to heal.

FAITH BRINGS HEALING

Jesus traveled on toward Jerusalem and passed through the border region between Samaria and Galilee. As he entered one village, ten men approached him, but they kept their distance, for they were lepers. They shouted to him, "Mighty Lord, our wonderful Master! Won't you have mercy on us and heal us?"

When Jesus stopped to look at them, he spoke these words: "Go to be examined by the Jewish priests."

They set off, and they were healed while walking along the way. One of them, a foreigner from Samaria, when he discovered that he was completely healed, turned back to find Jesus, shouting out joyous praises and glorifying God. When he found Jesus, he fell down at his feet and thanked him over and over, saying to him, "You are the Messiah." This man was a Samaritan.

"So where are the other nine?" Jesus asked. "Weren't there ten who were healed? They all refused to return to give thanks and give glory to God except you, a foreigner from Samaria?"

Then Jesus said to the healed man lying at his feet, "Arise and go. It was your faith that brought you salvation and healing." (Luke 17:11–19)

Jesus healed ten lepers and one returned to thank and praise Him. We see several instances of people expressing their gratitude to God after receiving their miracle.

After King Hezekiah was healed, he wrote a "psalm of praise" (Isaiah 38:9–22). The children sing praises in the temple after seeing Jesus heal the blind and the crippled (see Matthew 21:14). Mary sings her "Magnificat," her hymn of praise when she becomes impregnated by the Holy Spirit:

> *And Mary sang this song: "My soul is ecstatic, overflowing with praises to God! My spirit bursts with joy over my life-giving God! For he set his tender gaze upon me, his lowly servant girl. And from here on, everyone will know that I have been favored and blessed. The Mighty One has worked a mighty miracle for me; holy is his name! Mercy kisses all his godly lovers, from one generation to the next. Mighty power flows from him to scatter all those who walk in pride. Powerful princes he tears from their thrones and he lifts up the lowly to take their place. Those who hunger for him will always be filled, but the smug and self-satisfied he will send away empty. Because he can never forget to show mercy, he has helped his chosen servant, Israel, Keeping his promises to Abraham and to his descendants forever."* (Luke 1:46–55)

Miracles have always been and will always be about glorifying God. And yet, in the story of the ten lepers, only one returned to give thanks and praise—and he was a Samaritan, no less! Jesus received this one man's gratitude, but He didn't condemn the others. Condemnation is not from God. And note, He does not say, "Because you said 'thank you' you can keep your healing." No. He said, *"It was your faith that brought you salvation and healing"* (Luke 17:19).

Pastor Mark Batterson writes, "Gratitude is thanking God after He does it. Faith is thanking God before He does it." (Batterson, Chase the Lion: If Your Dream Doesn't Scare You, It's Too Small, 2016, 2019)

The Samaritan came to show gratitude to Jesus for his physical healing, but it was his faith that brought him there. And after showing his faith, Jesus healed the man even more completely—He gave him the gift of salvation.

Jesus also freely gave us the gift of salvation by what He did for us on the cross. Batterson says, "Our salvation, our healing, our deliverance—they were purchased, they were paid in full at Calvary's

Cross." They are already ours. Batterson says, "Stop praying for it, and start praising God for it." We don't have to pray for what is already ours. We can praise God for having already given it to us.

Batterson goes on to say, "Faith is celebrating in the present what God has already accomplished in the past and you know will happen in the future."

Even if you haven't yet received your healing, your deliverance, your salvation, it isn't because of a lack on God's part. Healing, deliverance, salvation—they were all already accomplished at the Cross. They are in the past! And because they are in the past, you can thank God for them now, knowing that you will receive them in your future.

Batterson believes,

"Prayer is asking God to do it (future tense). Praise is believing God has already done it (past tense). If you truly believe that He went to the Cross for your sins, that He bore all your sicknesses on His body, then you can sing praises to God now, even while you wait for your healing to manifest, knowing that it is always God's will to heal. If it wasn't, Jesus would have died for nothing. Instead, we know that Jesus died for everything!" (Batterson, *Chase the Lion: If Your Dream Doesn't Scare You, It's Too Small*, 2016, 2019)

DON'T BE DOUBLE-MINDED

On the third day Jesus left there and walked to the province of Galilee, where he was raised. Now Jesus knew that prophets are honored everywhere they go except in their own hometown. Even so, as Jesus arrived in the province of Galilee, he was welcomed by the people with open arms. Many of them had been in Jerusalem during the Passover Festival and had witnessed firsthand the miracles he had performed.

Jesus entered the village of Cana of Galilee where he had transformed water into wine. And there was a governmental official in Capernaum who had a son who was very sick and dying. When he heard that Jesus had left Judea and was staying in Cana of Galilee, he decided to make the journey to Cana. When he found Jesus he begged him, "You must come with me to Capernaum and heal my son!"

So Jesus said to him, "You never believe unless you see signs and wonders."

But the man continued to plead, "You have to come with me to Capernaum before my little boy dies!"

Then Jesus looked him in the eyes and said, "Go back home now. I promise you, your son will live and not die."

The man believed in his heart the words of Jesus and set off for home. When he was still a distance from Capernaum, his servants met him on the road and told him the good news, "Your son is healed! He's alive!"

Overjoyed, the father asked his servants, "When did my son begin to recover?"

"Yesterday," they said, "at one in the afternoon. All at once his fever broke—and now he's well!"

Then the father realized that it was at that very same hour that Jesus spoke the words to him, "Your son will live and not die." So from that day forward, the man and all his family and servants believed. This was Jesus's second extraordinary miracle in Galilee after coming from Judea. (John 4:43–54)

Scripture attests to the fact that we can stand in for others who need healing and we will see success. A little girl had faith, and Naaman was healed of leprosy. A group of friends had faith, and another member of their group got up and walked. A Centurion had faith, and his servant came back to life. And this man had faith for his son, who then recovered at the word of the Lord.

Yet, even though we can stand in for others who don't have the strength or belief to stand up for themselves, there is nothing like a personal faith in the Lord Jesus Christ.

Proverbs 22:6 says, *"Train up a child in the way he should go, Even when he is old he will not depart from it"* (NASB).

In his personal testimony regarding being healed as a child, Pastor Jack Hayford says:

> "I yearn for parents to learn to teach their children about the healing power of Jesus because once a child is healed by the power of Christ, no matter what happens in the years to come, that child will never forget that he is the Lord's. He will never forget that God touched him, that God has a private, personal investment in him, that God's healed him, and that God loves him." (Hayford, *www.jackhayford.org/teaching/articles/my-personal-testimony-of-healing/*)

After the little boy in the Scripture passage was healed, *"from that day forward, the man and all his family and servants believed"* (v. 53). This father didn't settle for vicarious faith. He wanted his entire family to believe, so he was sure that they knew who had healed his son. This is precisely Hayford's point—that as parents we need to tell our kids where their healing comes from. Then they will know that even when their time comes to leave home, they will be able to rely on God—for health, for success, for compassion, for power.

In 3 John 1:4 we read, "*It is the greatest joy of my life to hear that my children are consistently living their lives in the ways of truth!*" We are all children of God, regardless of our date of birth, and God delights when we believe "*in the ways of truth.*"

The father in the Scripture passage was not about to assume it was a coincidence that his son was feeling better by the time he returned home. He even sought confirmation by asking for the exact time that the child's fever broke. Don't fall into the trap of believing for healing and then becoming double-minded, wondering if it was really the power of God or if it was just happenstance.

> *Just make sure you ask empowered by confident faith without doubting that you will receive. For the ambivalent person believes one minute and doubts the next. Being undecided makes you become like the rough seas driven and tossed by the wind. You're up one minute and tossed down the next. When you are half-hearted and wavering it leaves you unstable. Can you really expect to receive anything from the Lord when you're in that condition?* (James 1:6–8)

A heart of doubt is less likely to see healing than a heart of faith. The father had unwavering, persistent faith that his son would be healed. And he was! The man's faith was rewarded with his son's healing, and the man responded by leading his entire family, servants and all, to a life of faith.

Healing glorifies God when He is given the credit, and when, through your testimony, others are brought into the household of faith.

RECEIVE WHAT YOU ALREADY HAVE IN JESUS

Then Jesus returned to Jerusalem to observe one of the Jewish holy days. Inside the city near the Sheep Gate there is a pool called in Aramaic, The House of Loving Kindness. And this pool is surrounded by five covered porches. Hundreds of sick people were lying there on the porches—the paralyzed, the blind, and the crippled, all of them waiting for their healing. For an angel of God would periodically descend into the pool to stir the waters, and the first one who stepped into the pool after the waters swirled would instantly be healed.

Now there was a man who had been disabled for thirty-eight years lying among the multitude of the sick. When Jesus saw him lying there, he knew that the man had been crippled for a long time. So Jesus said to him, "Do you truly long to be healed?"

The sick man answered him, "Sir, there's no way I can get healed, for I have no one who will lower me into the water when the angel comes. As soon as I try to crawl to the edge of the pool, someone else jumps in ahead of me."

Then Jesus said to him, "Stand up! Pick up your sleeping mat and you will walk!" Immediately he stood up—he was healed! So he rolled up his mat and walked again! Now this miracle took place on the Jewish Sabbath.

When the Jewish leaders saw the man walking along carrying his sleeping mat, they objected and said, "What are you doing carrying that? Don't you know it's the Sabbath? It's not lawful for you to carry things on the Sabbath!"

He answered them, "The man who healed me told me to pick it up and walk."

"What man?" they asked him. "Who was this man who ordered you to carry something on a Sabbath?" But the healed man couldn't give them an answer, for he didn't yet know who it was since Jesus had already slipped away into the crowd.

A short time later, Jesus found the man at the temple and said to him, "Look at you now! You're healed! Walk away from your sin so that nothing worse will happen to you."

Then the man went to the Jewish leaders to inform them, "It was Jesus who healed me!" (John 5:1–15)

Imagine this scene: hundreds of sick people, lying on five porches, and they all had their eyes on the pool, waiting for an angel to appear. They did not realize that Jesus was right there in their midst, walking amongst them. Throughout the Gospels people come in search of Jesus, and when they see Him, they cry out for His healing. But not one of these hundreds of sick people cried out to Him. Why? Because they weren't looking for Jesus. Their eyes were on the pool. And the man who had been an invalid for 38 years was no different. The difference was that Jesus saw him. JESUS SAW HIM! And He had a supernatural understanding of this man's affliction.

Jesus approached this man, but He doesn't seem to address him with the same compassion we are used to. In fact, He asks the man a question that seems a little rude, a little harsh. This man has been suffering for 38 years and Jesus has the gall to ask: *"Do you truly long to be healed?"* (John 5:6). *"Do you want to get well?"* (NIV). What is going on here?

According to Christine Caine:

"Jesus cares more about our healing than our feelings. Sometimes we care more about our feelings than our healing. We stop the healing of God based on what we are feeling. Sometimes we can even stop the healing in other people because we are so empathetic that we get right down with them in the pain and suffering that we forget that Jesus actually wants to heal them." (Caine, "Do You Want To Be Healed?")

Jesus could have sat down beside the man and commiserated with him. Jesus could have said, "What a bum rap you've gotten. Thirty-eight years! How unfair! How many people have you seen get in the pool in 38 years?" Or, Jesus could have said, "I'll sit here with you and watch for the angel. When that angel comes I'll throw you into the pool!" But Jesus already knew the man's heart. Jesus knew that the man was more focused on his feelings than on his healing. Just look at the man's response. When Jesus asked, "Do you truly long to be healed?" the man didn't respond with an emphatic "YES!"; he responded with blame. "*Do you truly long to be healed?*" Jesus asked (v. 6). "*There's no way I can ...*" the man answered (v. 7).

And his pity party doesn't end there. Not only is it everyone else's fault for not being there for him, but every time he tries "*someone else jumps in ahead of me*" (v.7). Someone else always gets his miracle.

After 38 years, this man had a "victim" mentality. He didn't even have it in him to say "yes" when Jesus asked if he wanted to be healed. But Jesus knew that health and healing is God's will. So instead of showing compassion, He showed power. Instead of empathizing, He pointed out the promise.

Healing wasn't in the water, and Jesus proved it! He didn't tell the man to go to the pool and wash like He told the blind man in John 9, or like Elisha told Naaman in 2 Kings 5. Jesus simply told him to get up. Why? Because He knew that if He put the man in the water, it would have confirmed to the man that the healing was in the water all along. But by telling him to get up, the man would see that the healing is in Jesus.

What can we learn from this story for our lives today? Christine Caine says:

"You will lie on your mat for your entire life if you don't look to Jesus and you keep blaming what someone else hasn't done for you or what someone else is getting before you." (Caine, "Do You Want To Be Healed?")

Don't give blame power over your healing. Fix your eyes on Jesus, and receive the healing that is already yours.

Do you hear that? Healing is ALREADY yours in Jesus. The footnote to The Passion Translation of John 5:6 says: "The Greek phrase *genesthai* is actually not a future tense ('want to be healed') but an aorist middle infinitive that indicates something already accomplished. Jesus is asking the crippled man if he is ready to abandon how he sees himself and now receive the faith for his healing."

The man was already healed. He just had to take his eyes off the pool and put them on Jesus to receive what was already his.

MODEL JESUS

So from that day forward the Jewish leaders began to persecute Jesus because of the things he did on the Sabbath.

Jesus answered his critics by saying, "Everyday my Father is at work, and I will be too!" This infuriated them and made them all the more eager to devise a plan to kill him. For not only did he break their Sabbath rules, but he called God "my Father," which made him equal to God.

So Jesus said, "I speak to you timeless truth. The Son is not able to do anything from himself or through my own initiative. I only do the works that I see the Father doing, for the Son does the same works as his Father.

"Because the Father loves his Son so much, he always reveals to me everything that he is about to do. And you will all be amazed when he shows me even greater works than what you've seen so far! For just like the Father has power to raise the dead, the Son will raise the dead and give life to whomever he wants.

"The Father now judges no one, for he has given all the authority to judge to the Son, so that the honor that belongs to the Father will now be shared with his Son. So if you refuse to honor the Son, you are refusing to honor the Father who sent him.

"I speak to you an eternal truth: if you embrace my message and believe in the One who sent me, you will never face condemnation, for in me, you have already passed from the realm of death into the realm of eternal life!"

"I speak to you eternal truth: Soon the dead will hear the voice of the Son of God, and those who listen will arise with life! For the Father has given the Son the power to impart life, even as the Father imparts life. The Father has transferred to the Son the authority to judge, because he is the Son of Man.

"So don't be amazed when I tell you these things, for there is a day coming when all who have ever died will hear my voice calling them back to life, and they will come out of their graves! Those who have done what is good will experience a resurrection to eternal life. And those who have practiced evil will taste the resurrection that brings them to condemnation!

"Nothing I do is from my own initiative, for as I hear the judgment passed by my Father, I execute judgment. And my judgments will be perfect, because I can do nothing on my own, except to fulfill the desires of my Father who sent me. For if I were to make claims about myself, you would have reasons to doubt. But there is another who bears witness on my behalf, and I know that what he testifies of me is true." (John 5:16–30)

Like John Wimber, Pastor Bill Johnson did not receive a special calling on his life to heal the sick, and yet both men have seen countless healings in their ministries. How? Johnson says, "While I had never had the 'call of God' encounter that others had, I did have the command of Scripture to '*heal the sick*' (Matthew 10:8). And that was enough." (Johnson, 2011) Wimber and Johnson are simply committed to heeding the commands of Scripture. Johnson writes:

"Believing that healing is either not for today, or that it is not a part of our salvation, is a flat-out lie. Believing a lie empowers the liar. Coming into agreement with the devil by believing a lie enables him to steal from us that much more easily. When we ignore or deny what God has provided, we lose the ability to discern the realms of the Holy Spirit and often wind up attributing the devil's work to God.

"The cost of tolerating lies is enormous. But spiritual falsehoods do not end with the lack of healing. Lies rob the heart of our natural ability to dream for more in our relationship with God. It makes fear king, while forcing us to live within the boundaries set by unbelief. While the quest for more of the miraculous makes many nervous, it is actually a sign of life. I refuse to listen to the warnings of possible excess from those satisfied with lack. The standard for the Christian life should not be set by those who have lost their ability to dream for the impossible. Pursuing the impossible is our nature in Christ." (Johnson, 2011)

One needn't look further than John 5 to see that the "impossible" was part of Jesus's daily life. To the people He said, "*you will all be amazed when he shows me even greater works than what you've seen so far*" (v. 20). All of those amazing works that Jesus did were based on what the Father did. Johnson says:

"Jesus only did what the Father was doing and only said what the Father was saying (see John 5:17–18; 8:26). This sets a pretty high standard for how to live. While Jesus is eternally God, He emptied Himself of His divinity and became a man (see Philippians 2:7). It is vital to note that He did all His miracles as a man, not as God. If He did them as God, I would still be impressed. But because He did them as a man yielded to God, I am now unsatisfied with my life, being compelled to follow the example He has given us. Jesus is the only model for us to follow." (Johnson, 2011)

Just as Jesus modeled His Father, we are to model Jesus—all for the glory of God.

IS SICKNESS THE RESULT OF SIN?

Afterward, as Jesus walked down the street, he noticed a man blind from birth. His disciples asked him, "Teacher, whose sin caused this guy's blindness, his own, or the sin of his parents?"

Jesus answered, "Neither. It happened to him so that you could watch him experience God's miracle. While I am with you, it is daytime and we must do the works of God who sent me while the light shines. For there is coming a dark night when no one will be able to work. As long as I am with you my life is the light that pierces the world's darkness."

Then Jesus spat on the ground and made some clay with his saliva. Then he anointed the blind man's eyes with the clay. And he said to the blind man, "Now go and wash the clay from your eyes in the ritual pool of Siloam." So he went and washed his face and as he came back, he could see for the first time in his life!

This caused quite a stir among the people of the neighborhood, for they noticed the blind beggar was now seeing! They began to say to one another, "Isn't this the blind man who once sat and begged?" Some said, "No, it can't be him!" Others said, "But it looks just like him—it has to be him!" All the while the man kept insisting, "I'm the man who was blind!"

Finally, they asked him, "What has happened to you?"

He replied, "I met the man named Jesus! He rubbed clay on my eyes and said, 'Go to the pool named Siloam and wash.'

So I went and while I was washing the clay from my eyes I began to see for the very first time ever!"

So the people of the neighborhood inquired, "Where is this man?"

"I have no idea." the man replied.

So the people marched him over to the Pharisees to speak with them. They were concerned because the miracle Jesus performed by making clay with his saliva and anointing the man's eyes happened on a Sabbath day, a day that no one was allowed to "work."

Then the Pharisees asked the man, "How did you have your sight restored?"

He replied, "A man anointed my eyes with clay, then I washed, and now I can see for the first time in my life!"

Then an argument broke out among the Pharisees over the healing of the blind man on the Sabbath. Some said, "This man who performed this healing is clearly not from God! He doesn't even observe the Sabbath!" Others said, "If Jesus is just an ordinary sinner, how could he perform a miracle like that?"

This prompted them to turn on the man healed of blindness, putting him on the spot in front of them all, demanding an answer. They asked, "Who do you say he is—this man who opened your blind eyes?"

"He's a prophet of God!" the man replied.

Still refusing to believe that the man had been healed and was truly blind from birth, the Jewish leaders called for the man's parents to be brought to them.

So they asked his parents, "Is this your son?"

"Yes," they answered.

"Was he really born blind?"

"Yes, he was," they replied.

So they pressed his parents to answer, "Then how is it that he's now seeing?"

"We have no idea," they answered. "We don't know what happened to our son. Ask him, he's a mature adult. He can speak for himself." (Now the parents were obviously intimidated by the Jewish religious leaders, for they had already announced to the people that if anyone publicly confessed Jesus as the Messiah, they would be excommunicated. That's why they told them, "Ask him, he's a mature adult. He can speak for himself.")

So once again they summoned the man who was healed of blindness and said to him, "Swear to God to tell us the truth! We know the man who healed you is a sinful man! Do you agree?"

The healed man replied, "I have no idea what kind of man he is. All I know is that I was blind and now I can see for the first time in my life!"

"But what did he do to you?" they asked. "How did he heal you?"

The man responded, "I told you once and you didn't listen to me. Why do you make me repeat it? Are you wanting to be his followers too?"

This angered the Jewish leaders. They heaped insults on him, "We can tell you are one of his followers—now we know it! We are true followers of Moses, for we know that God spoke to Moses directly. But as for this one, we don't know where he's coming from!"

131

"Well, what a surprise this is!" the man said. "You don't even know where he comes from, but he healed my eyes and now I can see! We know that God doesn't listen to sinners, but only to godly people who do his will. Yet who has ever heard of a man born blind that was healed and given back his eyesight? I tell you, if this man isn't from God, he wouldn't be able to heal me like he has!"

Some of the Jewish leaders were enraged and said, "Just who do you think you are to lecture us! You were born a blind, filthy sinner!" So they threw the man out in the street.

When Jesus learned they had thrown him out, he went to find him and said to him, "Do you believe in the Son of God?"

The man whose blind eyes were healed answered, "Who is he, Master? Tell me so that I can place all my faith in him."

Jesus replied, "You're looking right at him. He's speaking with you. It's me, the one in front of you now."

Then the man threw himself at his feet and worshiped Jesus and said, "Lord, I believe in you!"

And Jesus said, "I have come to judge those who think they see and make them blind. And for those who are blind, I have come to make them see."

Some of the Pharisees were standing nearby and overheard these words. They interrupted Jesus and said, "You mean to tell us that we are blind?"

Jesus told them, "If you would acknowledge your blindness, then your sin would be removed. But now that you claim to see, your sin remains with you!" (John 9:1–41)

In John 9:2, we see that the disciples wrestled with a delusion that continues to plague the Church today—they thought that the man's blindness was caused by sin. Jesus clears this up for the disciples, and our churches would do well to remember His words. Marilyn Hickey explains:

> "There are people who put a guilt trip on those who are ill by implying that their sickness is the result of some sin in their life. Remember that the sin principle which brought sickness and death is at work in the earth [and has been since the Fall]. Even babies are born with disease, deformity, or some physical or mental handicap, and those precious children have not had the opportunity to sin. Jesus, Himself, made it clear that it is not necessarily sin in an individual that causes their illness:
>
> *And as Jesus passed by, he saw a man which was blind from his birth. And his disciples asked him, saying, Master, who did sin, this man, or his parents, that he was born blind? Jesus answered, Neither hath this man sinned, nor his parents … (John 9:1–3 KJV).*
>
> "After telling His followers that it was neither the man nor his parents who had sinned, Jesus declared that the works of God should be made manifest in the man. The works of Satan had produced blindness, but God's work would bring healing and sight to the man. '*I must work the works of him that sent me,*' Jesus said; and then He proceeded to demonstrate that work (John 9:4 KJV). Bending over, the Lord spit on the ground, rolled a small amount of the wet dirt around in his fingers, and placed some of the 'clay' on each of the blind man's eyes. Jesus then commanded the man to go wash off the mud at the pool of Siloam.
>
> "It may have seemed a strange thing to do; but when the man exercised faith in Jesus and obeyed, he was given his sight. Jesus told His disciples—and He is still telling us today—that it wasn't blindness that brought glory to God, it was healing! Nowhere in the Scriptures do we ever see Jesus putting sickness or infirmity on anyone. Neither had God done such a thing so His Son could demonstrate either His power or the Father's power.

Although veiled in human flesh, Jesus was the image and expression of the Father. Jesus told the people that if they had seen Him, then they had seen the Father. If God puts sickness on people, then sometime, somewhere Jesus would have done the same." (Hickey)

But He never did. In fact, in the very next chapter, Jesus attests: "*The thief comes only to steal and kill and destroy; I have come that they may have life, and have it to the full*" (John 10:10 NIV).

HE HEARS YOUR TEARS

In the village of Bethany there was a man named Lazarus, and his sisters, Mary and Martha. Mary was the one who would anoint Jesus's feet with costly perfume and dry his feet with her long hair. One day Lazarus became very sick to the point of death. So his sisters sent a message to Jesus, "Lord, our brother Lazarus, the one you love, is very sick. Please come!"

When he heard this, he said, "This sickness will not end in death for Lazarus, but will bring glory and praise to God. This will reveal the greatness of the Son of God by what takes place."

Now even though Jesus loved Mary, Martha, and Lazarus, he remained where he was for two more days. Finally, on the third day, he said to his disciples, "Come. It's time to go to Bethany."

"But Teacher," they said to him, "do you really want to go back there? It was just a short time ago the people of Judea were going to stone you!"

Jesus replied, "Are there not twelve hours of daylight in every day? You can go through a day without the fear of stumbling when you walk in the One who gives light to the world. But you will stumble when the light is not in you, for you'll be walking in the dark."

Then Jesus added, "Lazarus, our friend, has just fallen asleep. It's time that I go and awaken him."

When they heard this, the disciples replied, "Lord, if he has just fallen asleep, then he'll get better." Jesus was speaking about Lazarus's death, but the disciples presumed he was talking about natural sleep.

Then Jesus made it plain to them, "Lazarus is dead. And for your sake, I'm glad I wasn't there, because now you have another opportunity to see who I am so that you will learn to trust in me. Come, let's go and see him."

So Thomas, nicknamed the Twin, remarked to the other disciples, "Let's go so that we can die with him."

Now when they arrived at Bethany, which was only about two miles from Jerusalem, Jesus found that Lazarus had already been in the tomb for four days. Many friends of Mary and Martha had come from the region to console them over the loss of their brother. And when Martha heard that Jesus was approaching the village, she went out to meet him, but Mary stayed in the house.

Martha said to Jesus, "My Lord, if only you had come sooner, my brother wouldn't have died. But I know that if you were to ask God for anything, he would do it for you."

Jesus told her, "Your brother will rise and live."

She replied, "Yes, I know he will rise with everyone else on resurrection day."

"Martha," Jesus said, "You don't have to wait until then. I am the Resurrection, and I am Life Eternal. Anyone who clings to me in faith, even though he dies, will live forever. And the one who lives by believing in me will never die. Do you believe this?"

Then Martha replied, "Yes, Lord, I do! I've always believed that you are the Anointed One, the Son of God who has come into the world for us!" Then she left and hurried off to her sister, Mary, and called her aside from all the mourners and whispered to her, "The Master is here and he's asking for you."

So when Mary heard this, she quickly went off to find him, for Jesus was lingering outside the village at the same spot where Martha met him. Now when Mary's friends who were comforting her noticed how quickly she ran out of the house, they followed her, assuming she was going to the tomb of her brother to mourn.

When Mary finally found Jesus outside the village, she fell at his feet in tears and said, "Lord, if only you had been here, my brother would not have died." When Jesus looked at Mary and saw her weeping at his feet, and all her friends who were with her grieving, he shuddered with emotion and was deeply moved with tenderness and compassion. He said to them, "Where did you bury him?"

"Lord, come with us and we'll show you," they replied.

Then tears streamed down Jesus's face.

Seeing Jesus weep caused many of the mourners to say, "Look how much he loved Lazarus." Yet others said, "Isn't this the One who opens blind eyes? Why didn't he do something to keep Lazarus from dying?"

Then Jesus, with intense emotions, came to the tomb—a cave with a stone placed over its entrance. Jesus told them, "Roll away the stone."

Then Martha said, "But Lord, it's been four days since he died—by now his body is already decomposing!"

Jesus looked at her and said, "Didn't I tell you that if you will believe in me, you will see God unveil his power?"

So they rolled away the heavy stone. Jesus gazed into heaven and said, "Father, thank you that you have heard my prayer, for you listen to every word I speak. Now, so that these who stand here with me will believe that you have sent me to the earth as your messenger, I will use the power you have given me." Then with a loud voice Jesus shouted with authority: "Lazarus! Come out of the tomb!"

Then in front of everyone, Lazarus, who had died four days earlier, slowly hobbled out—he still had grave clothes tightly wrapped around his hands and feet and covering his face! Jesus said to them, "Unwrap him and let him loose."

From that day forward many of those who had come to visit Mary believed in him, for they had seen with their own eyes this amazing miracle! (John 11:1–45)

John 11:35 (NIV): "*Jesus wept.*" Why would Jesus weep if He knew He was about to raise Lazarus from the dead?

Pastor Creflo Dollar points to another Scripture to help us see what is truly going on here. Romans 8:26 (NIV): "*We do not know what we ought to pray for, but the Spirit himself intercedes for us through wordless groans.*" When we don't know what to pray, when we don't know how to pray, when we are so overcome with emotion, the Holy Spirit intercedes for us. Dollar says, "*The heart is so full it takes the expression of groaning and weeping.*" (Dollar, Dimensions to Praying in the Spirit) Weeping. Jesus wept. John 11:33 says, Jesus "*shuddered with emotion.*" The MEV says, Jesus "*groaned in the spirit.*" Groaning and weeping. Do you see what is going on here? Jesus wasn't crying. He was praying.

Pastor Dollar says praying in the Spirit "is one of the deepest dimensions of prayer that a believer has authority to pray." In John 11:37, onlookers were wondering why Jesus, who opens blind eyes, wasn't doing anything. But He was doing everything—He was groaning and weeping and receiving power to raise the dead. In verse 41 Jesus says, "*Father, thank you that you have heard my prayer.*" Nowhere in this passage does it say "Jesus prayed." But it does say, "*Jesus wept.*"

HE IS OUR GREAT PHYSICIAN

One afternoon Peter and John went to the temple for the three o'clock prayer. As they came to the entrance called the Beautiful Gate, they were captured by the sight of a man crippled from birth being carried and placed at the entrance to the temple. He was often brought there to beg for money from those going in to worship. When he noticed Peter and John going into the temple, he begged them for money.

Peter and John, looking straight into the eyes of the crippled man, said, "Look at us!" Expecting a gift, he readily gave them his attention. Then Peter said, "I don't have money, but I'll give you this—by the power of the name of Jesus Christ of Nazareth, stand up and walk!"

Peter held out his right hand to the crippled man. As he pulled the man to his feet, suddenly power surged into his crippled feet and ankles. The man jumped up, stood there for a moment stunned, and then began to walk around! As he went into the temple courts with Peter and John, he leapt for joy and shouted praises to God.

When all the people saw him jumping up and down and heard him glorifying God, they realized it was the crippled beggar they had passed by in front of the Beautiful Gate. Astonishment swept over the crowd, for they were amazed over what had happened to him.

Dumbfounded over what they were witnessing, the crowd ran over to Peter and John, who were standing under the covered walkway called Solomon's Porch. Standing there also was the healed beggar, clinging to Peter and John.

With the crowd surrounding him, Peter said to them all, "People of Israel, listen to me! Why are you so amazed by this healing? Why do you stare at us? We didn't make this crippled man walk by our own power or authority. The God of our ancestors, Abraham, Isaac, and Jacob, has done this. For he has glorified his Servant Jesus, the one you denied to Pilate's face when he decided to release him—and you insisted that he be crucified. You rejected the one who is holy and righteous, and instead begged for a murderer to be released. You killed the Prince of Life! But God raised him from the dead, and we stand here as witnesses to that fact. Faith in Jesus's name has healed this man standing before you. It is the faith that comes through believing in Jesus's name that has made the crippled man walk right in front of your eyes!

"My fellow Jews, I realize that neither you nor your leaders realize the grave mistake you made. But in spite of what you've done, God has fulfilled what he foretold through the prophets long ago about the sufferings of his Anointed One. And now you must repent and turn back to God so that your sins will be removed, and so that times of refreshing will stream from the Lord's presence. And he will send you Jesus, the Messiah, the chosen one for you. For he must remain in heaven until the restoration of all things has taken place, fulfilling everything that God said long ago through his holy prophets. For has not Moses told us:

> 'The Lord your God will raise up a prophet from among you who is like me. Listen to him and follow everything he tells you. Every person who disobeys that prophet will be cut off and completely destroyed.'

"In fact, every prophet from the time of Samuel onward has prophesied of these very days! And you are heirs of their prophecies and of the covenants God made with your fathers when he promised Abraham, 'Your descendant will bring blessing to all the people on the earth.'

"Now that God raised up his Son, he has chosen to send him first to you that he might bless you by turning each one of you from your wickedness." (Acts 3:1–26)

The first miracle recorded in the book of Acts, after Jesus's resurrection and ascension into heaven, was the healing of this crippled man at the gate called "Beautiful." The man had been crippled since birth, unable to walk. But he had friends who would occasionally bring him to the temple so he could beg for food, money, whatever church-goers were willing to give him.

Peter and John were *"captured"* by the man (v. 2) and instantly knew what God was going to do. They asked the man to look them square in the eye, and they must have seen something there. They must have seen faith there in the depths of his soul.

Unfortunately, they had no money for the man, and no food. But Peter offered something better: *"I don't have money, but I'll give you this—by the power of the name of Jesus Christ of Nazareth, stand up and walk!"* (v. 6). Power surged through the man, into his feet and ankles, when Peter gripped his hand (Peter is the great power surger!; see also Acts 5:15). The man *"jumped up"*—stunned. Then he *"leapt"* for joy and sang praises. The people couldn't believe what they were seeing: the crippled man was *"jumping up and down"* and they *"heard him glorifying God"* (v. 9). They were astonished. They were amazed. They were dumbfounded. Wasn't this the man who had been crippled from birth? Wasn't this the man they gave their loose change to on Sunday mornings? Wasn't this the man they carried to the Beautiful Gate so he could beg? And now here he was, walking and leaping and shouting!

Everyone ran to Peter and John. How would these men explain what the people were seeing? And Peter began to preach:

People of Israel, listen to me! Why are you so amazed by this healing? Why do you stare at us? We didn't make this crippled man walk by our own power or authority. The God of our ancestors, Abraham, Isaac, and Jacob, has done this ... Faith in Jesus's name has healed this man standing before you. It is the faith that comes through believing in

Jesus's name that has made the crippled man walk right in front of your eyes! (Acts 3:12–13,16)

They immediately gave credit where credit was due. Pastor Bill Johnson writes:

> "It is important for us to understand that it is always God who heals. Sometimes we get to deliver the package. Sometimes we watch Him deliver the package Himself." (Johnson, 2011)

God will often use His people in healing, as He did with Peter and John in Acts 3, but it is essential to remember that "it is always God who heals."

Johnson also points out that the man received total healing:

> "Remember the man who was healed at the Gate Beautiful? Scripture tells us he walked, leaped, and praised God. He was touched in every area. He was physically healed—he walked. He was emotionally healed—he leaped. He was also spiritually healed—he praised God." (Johnson, 2011)

God cares about your physical body, your emotional health, and your spiritual life. Jesus died so that you could be healthy and whole in ALL aspects of your being!

WORKS CITED

Batterson, Mark. 2014. *The Grave Robber: How Jesus Can Make Your Impossible Possible.* Grand Rapids, MI: Baker Books, a division of Baker Publishing Group.

—. 2016, 2019. *Chase the Lion: If Your Dream Doesn't Scare You, It's Too Small.* New York: Multnomah, an imprint of the Crown Publishing Group, a division of Penguin Random House LLC.

Bevere, John. 2019. *Honor's Reward: Unlocking the Power of the Forgotten Virtue.* Palmer Lake, CO: Messenger International, Inc.

Bickle, Mike. "The Authority of the Believer: Standing in our Healing". *https://mikebickle.org.edge-suite.net/MikeBickleVOD/2009/20091129_Authority_of_Believer-Standing_in_our_Healing.pdf.*

—. "Defining True Discipleship". *https://mikebickle.org/?search=heal.*

—. "Jesus's Unique Power and Compassion". *https://mikebickle.org/?search=heal.*

Caine, Christine. n.d. "Do You Want To Be Healed?" Equip & Empower, TBN.

Johnson, Bill and Randy Clark. 2011. *The Essential Guide to Healing: Equipping All Christians to Pray for the Sick.* Grand Rapids, Michigan: Chosen Books, a division of Baker Publishing Group.

Clark, Randy. 2015. *Power to Heal: Keys to Activating God's Healing Power in Your Life.* Shippensburg, PA: Destiny Image Publications, Inc.

Dollar, Creflo. n.d. "Dimensions to Praying in the Spirit".

—. 2014. *Overcoming Fear: Eliminating the Bondage of Fear.*

College Park, Georgia: Creflo Dollar Ministries.

Fontaine, Leon. n.d. "Living A Miraculous Life". The Spirit Contemporary Life.

Hayford, Jack. "My Personal Testimony of Healing". *www.jackhayford.org/teaching/articles/my-personal-testimony-of-healing/*

Hickey, Marilyn. 1992. *Be Healed.*

Jeremiah, David. 2018. *Overcomer: 8 Ways to Live a Life of Unstoppable Strength, Unmovable Faith, and Unbelievable Power.* Nashville, Tennessee: W Publishing, an imprint of Thomas Nelson.

Kilpatrick, John. "Door to Blessings ". *http://johnkilpatrick. org/media/player/media/door-to-the-blessings/video/.*

Lawrence, Peter H. 2011. *The Spirit Who Speaks: God's Supernatural Intervention in Your Life.* Colorado Springs, CO: David C. Cook.

Morris, Robert. n.d. "My Christian Calling" from the "Why Am I Here" sermon series. Gateway Church, Southlake, TX.

Munroe, Miles. 2002. *The Purpose and Power of Love & Marriage.* Shippensburg, PA: Destiny Image Publications, Inc.

Prince, Joseph. "Come As You Are and Receive Your Miracle". Sermon by Joseph Prince. New Creation Church, Singapore.

—. n.d. "Live Healed". New Creation Church, Singapore.

—. 2012. *Healing Promises*. Lake Mary, Florida: Charisma House.

Wimber, John. 2006. *The Way In is the Way On.* Boise, ID: Ampelon Publishing.

APPENDIX—COMMUNION

From Joseph Prince's book, *Healing Promises*:

"When you remember how Jesus willingly came to save you and suffered for your healing at the cross, it will cast out every fear of not receiving healing from Him. That's what partaking of the Holy Communion is about. When you hold the bread in your hand, simply remember how Jesus's body was broken at the cross so that yours may be healed and whole. Say, 'Lord Jesus, thank You for bearing my condition on Your own body at the cross. When the lashes fell across Your back, my condition died. It has no right to linger in my body!' Likewise, when you partake of the cup, remember that Jesus shed His blood to save you. Say, 'Jesus, thank You for Your shed blood that has washed away my sins and made me righteous. Because I am righteous in Your sight, healing belongs to me. I receive Your healing and resurrection life for my body right now.' Beloved, remember the Lord and partake your way to divine health!" (Prince, J. *Healing Promises*. 2012.)

As they ate, Jesus took the bread and blessed it and broke it and gave it to his disciples. He said to them, "This is my body. Eat it." Then taking the cup of wine and giving praises to the Father, he entered into covenant with them, saying, "This is my blood. Each of you must drink it in fulfillment of the covenant. For this is the blood that seals the new covenant. It will be poured out for many for the complete forgiveness of sins. The next time we drink this, I will be with you and we will drink it together with a new understanding in the kingdom realm of my Father."

Then they sang a psalm and left for the Mount of Olives.
(Matthew 26:26–30)

Every believer was faithfully devoted to following the teachings of the apostles. Their hearts were mutually linked to one another, sharing communion and coming together regularly for prayer. A deep sense of holy awe swept over everyone, and the apostles performed many miraculous signs and wonders. All the believers were in fellowship as one body, and they shared with one another whatever they had. Out of generosity they even sold their assets to distribute the proceeds to those who were in need among them. Daily they met together in the temple courts and in one another's homes to celebrate communion. They shared meals together with joyful hearts and tender humility. They were continually filled with praises to God, enjoying the favor of all the people. And the Lord kept adding to their number daily those who were coming to life. (Acts 2:42–47)

When the uproar finally died down, Paul gathered the believers and encouraged their hearts. He kissed them, said good-bye, and left for Macedonia. At every place he passed through, he brought words of great comfort and encouragement to the believers. Then he went on to Greece and stayed there for three months.

Just as Paul was about to sail for Syria, he learned of a plot against him by the Jews, so he decided to return by going through Macedonia. Seven men accompanied him as far as western Turkey. They were Sopater, son of Pyrrhus from Berea, Aristarchus and Secundus from Thessalonica, Gaius from Derbe, and Timothy, Tychicus, and Trophimus from western Turkey. These men went ahead and were waiting for us at Troas. As soon as all of the Passover celebrations were over, we sailed from Philippi. After five days we joined the others in Troas, where we stayed another week. On Sunday we gathered to take communion and to hear Paul preach. Because he was planning to leave the next day, he continued speaking until past midnight. Many flickering lamps burned in the upstairs chamber where we were meet-

ing. Sitting in an open window listening was a young man named Eutychus. As Paul's sermon dragged on, Eutychus became drowsy and fell into a deep slumber. Sound asleep, he fell three stories to his death below.

Paul went downstairs, bent over the boy, and embraced him. Taking him in his arms, he said to all the people gathered, "Stop your worrying. He's come back to life!"

Paul went back upstairs, served communion, and ate a meal with them. Then he picked back up where he left off and taught until dawn. Filled with enormous joy, they took the boy home alive and everyone was encouraged. (Acts 20:1–12)

My cherished friends, keep on running far away from idolatry. I know I am writing to thoughtful people, so carefully consider what I say. For when we pray for the blessing of the communion cup, isn't this our co-participation with the blood of Jesus? And the bread that we distribute, isn't this the bread of our co-participation with the body of Christ? For although we're many, we become one loaf of bread and one body as we feast together on one loaf.

Consider the people of Israel when they fell into idolatry. When they ate the sacrifices offered to the gods, weren't they becoming communal participants in what was sacrificed? Now, am I saying that idols and the sacrifices offered to them have any value? Absolutely not! However, I am implying that when an unbeliever offers a sacrifice to an idol, it is not offered to the true God but to a demon. I don't want you to be participants with demons! You can't drink from the cup of the Lord and the cup of demons. You can't feast at the table of the Lord and feast at the table of demons. Who would ever want to arouse the Lord's jealousy? Is that something you think you're strong enough to endure? (1 Corinthians 10:14–22)

Now, on this next matter, I wish I could commend you, but I cannot, because when you meet together as a church family it is doing more harm than good! I've been told many times that when you meet as a congregation, divisions and cliques emerge—and to some extent, this doesn't surprise me. Differences of opinion are unavoidable, yet they will reveal which ones among you truly have God's approval.

When all of your house churches gather as one church family, you are not really properly celebrating the Lord's Supper. For when it comes time to eat, some gobble down their food before anything is given to others—one is left hungry while others become drunk! Don't you all have homes where you can eat and drink? Don't you realize that you're showing a superior attitude by humiliating those who have nothing? Are you trying to show contempt for God's beloved church? How should I address this appropriately? If you're looking for my approval, you won't find it!

I have handed down to you what came to me by direct revelation from the Lord himself. The same night in which he was handed over, he took bread and gave thanks. Then he distributed it to the disciples and said, "Take it and eat your fill. It is my body, which is given for you. Do this to remember me." He did the same with the cup of wine after supper and said, "This cup seals the new covenant with my blood. Drink it—and whenever you drink this, do it to remember me."

Whenever you eat this bread and drink this cup, you are retelling the story, proclaiming our Lord's death until he comes. For this reason, whoever eats the bread or drinks the cup of the Lord in the wrong spirit will be guilty of dishonoring the body and blood of the Lord. So let each individual first evaluate his own attitude and only then eat the bread and drink the cup. For continually eating and drinking with a wrong spirit will bring judgment upon yourself by not recognizing the body. This insensitivity is why many of you are weak, chronically ill, and some even dying. If you do not sit in judgment of others, you will avoid judgment yourself. But when we are judged, it is the Lord's training so that we will not be condemned along with the world.

So then, my fellow believers, when you assemble as one to share a meal, show respect for one another and wait for all to be served. If you are that hungry, eat at home first, so that when you gather together you will not bring judgment upon yourself. When I come to you, I will answer the other questions you asked me in your letter. (1 Corinthians 11:17–34)